# Windows Vista
*Pocket Reference*

# Windows Vista
## *Pocket Reference*

*Preston Gralla*

O'REILLY®

Beijing · Cambridge · Farnham · Köln · Paris · Sebastopol · Taipei · Tokyo

**Windows Vista Pocket Reference**
by Preston Gralla

Copyright © 2007 Preston Gralla. All rights reserved.
Printed in the United States of America.

Published by O'Reilly Media, Inc., 1005 Gravenstein Highway North,
Sebastopol, CA 95472.

O'Reilly books may be purchased for educational, business, or sales
promotional use. Online editions are also available for most titles
(*safari.oreilly.com*). For more information, contact our corporate/
institutional sales department: (800) 998-9938 or *corporate@oreilly.com*.

**Editor:** Brian Jepson

**Production Editor:**
  Rachel Monaghan

**Copyeditor:** Audrey Doyle

**Proofreader:** Rachel Monaghan

**Indexer:** John Bickelhaupt

**Cover Designer:** Karen Montgomery

**Interior Designer:** David Futato

**Illustrators:** Robert Romano and
  Jessamyn Read

**Printing History:**
  February 2007:          First Edition.

Nutshell Handbook, the Nutshell Handbook logo, and the O'Reilly logo are
registered trademarks of O'Reilly Media, Inc. The *Pocket Reference* series
designations, *Windows Vista Pocket Reference*, the image of a European
common frog, and related trade dress are trademarks of O'Reilly Media, Inc.

Many of the designations used by manufacturers and sellers to distinguish
their products are claimed as trademarks. Where those designations appear
in this book, and O'Reilly Media, Inc. was aware of a trademark claim, the
designations have been printed in caps or initial caps.

While every precaution has been taken in the preparation of this book, the
publisher and author assume no responsibility for errors or omissions, or for
damages resulting from the use of the information contained herein.

ISBN-10: 0-596-52808-6
ISBN-13: 978-0-596-52808-9
[C]

# Contents

# Introduction

This pocket reference is intended to provide the information
Windows Vista users need most often in a quick and concise
format. This tiny volume is small enough to fit in your
pocket or laptop case, yet it is packed with hundreds of tips,
shortcuts, and other tidbits of information that will make
Windows Vista easier to use.

Less-experienced Windows Vista users should turn to the
brief crash course in Chapter 1 of the book. If you're a
hands-on learner, you should be able to pick up any of the
concepts discussed there in no time at all. Chapter 2 lists
dozens of keyboard and mouse shortcuts available for every
aspect of Windows Vista, and Chapter 3 provides a listing of
the most useful components, features, and settings that make
up Windows Vista—an encyclopedia of everything you can
do with Windows out of the box. Chapter 4 highlights how
to use the Registry, along with several Registry hacks, while
Chapter 5 documents the most important command-line
prompts and how to use them.

Anyone wishing to learn more will benefit from the additional background and details provided by full-size books
such as my recently published book, *Windows Vista in a Nutshell*, also available from O'Reilly.

# Conventions Used in This Book

The following typographical conventions are used in this book:

`Constant width`
> Used to indicate anything to be typed, as well as command-line computer output, code examples, Registry keys, and keyboard accelerators (discussed below).

**`Constant width bold`**
> Used to indicate user input.

`Constant width italic`
> Used to indicate variables in examples and so-called "replaceable" text. For instance, to open a document in Notepad from the command line, you'd type `notepad filename`, where `filename` is the full path and name of the document you wish to open.

*[Square brackets]*
> Square brackets around an option (usually a command-line parameter) mean that the parameter is optional. Parameters and keywords not shown in square brackets are typically mandatory. If you see two or more options separated by the | character, it means that they are mutually exclusive; only one or the other can be specified, but not both.

*Italic*
> Used to introduce new terms and to indicate URLs, variables in text, file and folder/directory names, and UNC pathnames.

Rather than using procedural steps to tell you how to reach a given Windows Vista user interface element or application, I use a shorthand path notation. For example:

> Start → Programs → Accessories → Calculator

means "Open the Start menu (on the Desktop), then choose Programs, then choose Accessories, and then click Calculator." The path is always relative to a well-known location, such as the following:

*Control Panel*
> Start → Control Panel (in the Windows Vista-style Start menu)
>
> Start → Settings → Control Panel (in the Classic Start menu)

*My Computer, My Network Places, Recycle Bin*
> The familiar Desktop icons by these names, any of which may or may not be visible, depending on your settings

*Start*
> The Start button on the Taskbar

*Windows Explorer/Explorer*
> The two-pane folder view, commonly referred to as simply "Explorer": Start → Programs → Accessories → System Tools → Windows Explorer

*xxxx menu*
> Menu *xxxx* in the application currently being discussed (e.g., File, Edit)

Note that the elements of the Control Panel may or may not be divided into categories, depending on context and a setting on your computer. So, rather than a cumbersome explanation of this unfortunate design every time the Control Panel comes up, the following notation is used:

> Control Panel → [Performance and Maintenance] → Scheduled Tasks

where the category (in this case, Performance and Maintenance) is shown in square brackets, implying that you may or may not encounter this step.

# We'd Like to Hear from You

Please address comments and questions concerning this book to the publisher:

> O'Reilly Media, Inc.
> 1005 Gravenstein Highway North
> Sebastopol, CA 95472
> 800-998-9938 (in the U.S. or Canada)
> 707-829-0515 (international/local)
> 707-829-0104 (fax)

There is a web page for this book, which lists errata, examples, or any additional information. You can access this page at:

> *http://www.oreilly.com/catalog/9780596528089*

To comment or ask technical questions about this book, send email to:

> *bookquestions@oreilly.com*

For more information about our books, conferences, resource centers, and the O'Reilly Network, see the O'Reilly web site at:

> *http://www.oreilly.com*

# CHAPTER 1

# A Crash Course in the Basics

The following brief sections tell you what's new in Windows Vista, illustrate the layout of the Windows Vista interface, and identify the important concepts and components. Continue to Chapter 2 for tips and shortcuts for working with files, windows, and applications.

## What's New in Windows Vista

Windows Vista is a significant rework of Windows, and although the basics of Windows are the same, much has changed. Here are the most significant additions and changes in Windows Vista compared to Windows XP:

*Windows Aero interface*

The new interface is the first thing people will notice when they see Windows Vista on a Vista Premium-ready system. It sports customizable, translucent windows (called *Aero Glass*); live Taskbar thumbnails that show a live preview of an underlying window when a mouse is held over the tile; and Windows Flip and Windows Flip 3D, which show thumbnails of open windows as you flip through them. As the name implies, Windows Flip 3D, shown in Figure 1-1, shows the thumbnails in three dimensions. Note that Windows Aero is not available on the least expensive versions of Windows Vista, and that it has special hardware requirements. There are three other levels of the interface that are less sophisticated than Windows Aero: Windows Classic, Basic, and Standard.

*Figure 1-1. Using Flip 3D to flip through live previews of open windows*

*Security*

Security has been enhanced at every level of the operating system, in both visible and invisible ways. Windows Defender protects against spyware, and the Windows Firewall now includes outbound as well as inbound protection. (By default, though, outbound protection is turned off.) Internet Explorer runs by default in Protected Mode, which protects the operating system from assault via the browser, and it includes a phishing filter. Windows Service Hardening stops background Windows services from being used by malware to damage the filesystem, Registry, or network to which the PC is connected. Windows Vista also gives network administrators more control over network and PC security, such as the ability to restrict access to removable storage devices such as Universal Serial Bus (USB) flash drives. Parental Controls allow parents to determine how their children can use the computer and what content they can access. BitLocker Drive Encryption, when used with compatible hardware, locks down a hard disk so that it cannot be accessed if the computer is stolen. Windows Vista also includes User Account Control (UAC), which pops up warnings and asks for passwords when certain setup or customization screens or features are accessed. This enhances security, but it can also mean that you will have to type in a password or click an approval button before you can change certain system features.

*Revised Internet Explorer*

Internet Explorer, shown in Figure 1-2, has been given its most significant overhaul in years, with the addition of tabs, a redesigned menu system, increased security, Instant Search via an integrated search bar, page zoom, and better printing.

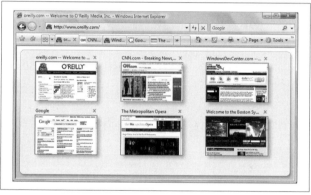

*Figure 1-2. A revamped Internet Explorer, featuring tabs and a redesigned menu system*

*RSS support*

Really Simple Syndication (RSS) allows for the delivery of live feeds of web content, news, and web logs. Internet Explorer includes a built-in RSS reader that lets you subscribe to and read RSS feeds.

*Windows Sidebar and Gadgets*

The new Windows Sidebar, shown in Figure 1-3, puts information and  frequently used tasks directly on the desktop. Gadgets that live on the Sidebar perform tasks such as fetching RSS feeds, displaying system information, and showing up-to-date stock information.

*Better search*

Search speed has been significantly increased, integrated throughout the operating system, and enhanced with more ways to find files, programs, email, and web information. The Instant Search feature, in Windows Explorer and on the Search menu, finds information the instant you start typing. Instant Search is context-sensitive, so when a search is performed from within a folder, it will search that folder. A new Search Pane adds simple ways to fine-tune and filter searches. In addition, you can create Virtual Folders that are based on search criteria—for example, you can create a Virtual Folder that constantly updates itself and that will display all *.doc* files over a certain size, created after a certain date, and containing certain words.

*New "Centers"*

Windows Vista organizes common tasks and features into *Centers*, which contain all the information and settings related to the task or feature. For example, the Network and Sharing Center, shown in Figure 1-4, allows you to view information about your current network and connection, see a complete network map, connect to new networks, customize your connections, turn file sharing on or off, change security settings, and so on. Similarly, the Windows Mobility Center includes settings and information related to mobile computing. And the Backup and Restore Center makes it easy for you to back up and restore data as well as the current state of your computer.

*Figure 1-3. The Windows Sidebar, which contains gadgets that perform a wide variety of tasks, as well as gather live information*

*Figure 1-4. The Network and Sharing Center: command central for network information and configuration*

### New networking features

Collaboration tools make it easy for people to find others with whom to have live meetings over a network. Wireless networking includes support for the WPA2/802.11i security standards. Windows Vista also supports the new IPv6 Transmission Control Protocol/Internet Protocol (TCP/IP) architecture, which expands the number of available IP addresses.

### Improved multimedia

Windows Media Center has been overhauled. If a PC has a TV tuner, it will be able to record, watch, and pause live television feeds. Browsing, searching for, and organizing digital media such as photos and music have been improved. See the upcoming "Windows Vista Editions" section of this chapter for details on which versions of Vista support these functions. In addition, Windows Media Player 11 features plenty of improvements.

## Faster startup and resume

Whenever Windows Vista starts up, it has to run a variety of scripts and services, just as earlier versions of Windows had to do. But with Vista, startup doesn't wait for those scripts and services; instead, it moves ahead and starts, and the scripts run in the background, leading to faster startup. To make Windows Vista start even faster, you can put it into Sleep Mode rather than shutting it down. In Sleep Mode, all your open documents, windows, and programs are saved, but the computer shuts down most of its functions. When you wake it from Sleep Mode, the documents, windows, and programs are restored in exactly the state they were in when your computer went to sleep. Waking from Sleep Mode happens within seconds—faster than it takes for a computer to start up from a shutdown.

## SuperFetch

This new technology can improve your PC's performance by watching the programs and data you often use, and then fetching them before you actually need them. That way, the programs and data load and run much faster when you open them. SuperFetch really comes into its own when combined with ReadyBoost, which allows your PC to use a high-speed flash drive for a SuperFetch cache. Flash drives are much less expensive than RAM, so this is an inexpensive way to boost your PC's performance. In addition, some systems, such as laptops, may have limited RAM capacity, so a flash drive is a way to boost those systems' performance.

## Restart Manager

Under earlier versions of Windows, you frequently had to reboot your PC whenever you installed a patch to a program because Windows was unable to shut down all the processes associated with that program. With Windows Vista, you will have to reboot far less frequently when applying a patch because Restart Manager can more effectively close down and restart the required processes. (Note that Restart Manager is not an application that you use directly; instead, it's a kind of internal plumbing that works without your intervention.)

*Improved stability*

Windows Vista includes a variety of new features under the hood to make it more reliable and less prone to crashes than previous versions of Windows. The Startup Repair Tool automatically fixes common startup problems, and all Windows services now have recovery policies that allow Vista to automatically restart a service that has crashed, as well as restart associated services.

*Better backup*

It's no secret that the backup programs built into Windows XP Home and Professional left much to be desired, and because of that, they were rarely used. Windows Vista's new backup program, Windows Backup, is actually useful and lets you back up to writable discs, USB flash drives, and other removable media, as well as across a network. Backups can be completely automated, and you can also back up an entire system image (what Windows Vista calls a *Complete PC backup*) that saves the current state of your PC so that it can be easily restored in the case of a system failure, or if your PC is stolen. There's also a Backup and Restore Center, shown in Figure 1-5, which provides a central location for all backup and restoration chores.

# Windows Vista Editions

Those who were slightly confused by the two different versions of Windows XP—the Home Edition and the Professional Edition—will be flummoxed by the dizzying array of different Windows Vista versions. There are five different core Vista versions, for everyone from users with bare-bones PCs, to home users interested in multimedia, to users who work in

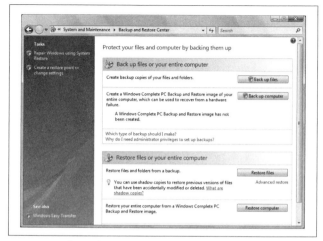

*Figure 1-5. The Backup and Restore Center*

large enterprises. As a practical matter, though, most home users will end up with Windows Vista Home Premium; those in many businesses will end up with Windows Vista Business; and those in very large corporations will run Windows Vista Enterprise Edition. Here's the rundown on the five core versions and how they differ:

*Windows Vista Home Basic*

As the name implies, this edition offers only bare-bones features. It's designed to run on entry-level PCs and doesn't have the Windows Aero interface, doesn't support creating video DVDs, and lacks Media Center features. It is missing more as well, such as mobility features, and it doesn't support Tablet PCs. Most likely, few people will opt for this version of Windows Vista.

*Windows Vista Business*

This version is aimed at users in small to medium-size businesses. It includes Windows Aero, supports Tablet PCs, and has most other Vista features. But it doesn't have a variety of multimedia features, such as the capability to create and burn video DVDs. It does, though, have a variety of features aimed at IT staff, such as wireless network provisioning capabilities, Remote Desktop connections, image-based backup, and other network administration features.

*Windows Vista Home Premium*

This has Aero and supports all of the multimedia Vista features, such as creating video DVDs, slide show creation, and the Windows Media Center. It supports basic networking and wireless networking, but it doesn't have network administration tools, wireless network provisioning, or the capability to connect to a domain. It also doesn't have the Encrypting File System (EFS) or image-based backup.

*Windows Vista Enterprise Edition*

This one is for large enterprises, and only businesses that have Microsoft Software Assurance or a Microsoft Enterprise Agreement get this version. It offers everything that Windows Vista Business does, and it includes hardware-based encryption, called *BitLocker Drive Encryption*, which employs a physical hardware key and a passcode to secure volumes. This version also comes as a single image that enterprises can deploy from a central location.

*Windows Vista Ultimate*

Like the name says, this is the Mother of All Vistas. It has all the features and tools in every other version of Vista—the networking and administrative tools of the various business editions, and the multimedia features of the home editions.

Note that there are actually eight Vista versions. The remaining three versions will be sold only outside the United States. The Windows Vista Starter edition will be sold only on low-end PCs in emerging markets, and two "N" versions of Vista are required to be sold in the European Union. The N versions lack some media-related features.

Table 1-1 provides more detailed information about the different Vista versions, as well as where to turn to learn more.

*Table 1-1. Comparing selected features in various versions of Windows Vista*

| Feature | Home Basic | Home Premium | Business | Enterprise Edition | Ultimate |
|---|---|---|---|---|---|
| Windows Aero | No | Yes | Yes | Yes | Yes |
| Parental Controls | Yes | Yes | No | No | Yes |
| Windows DVD Maker | No | Yes | No | No | Yes |
| Tablet PC features | No | Yes | Yes | Yes | Yes |
| Remote Desktop | Client only | Client only | Host and client | Host and client | Host and client |
| Automated backup | No | Yes | Yes | Yes | Yes |
| Back up to a network device or folder | No | Yes | Yes | Yes | Yes |
| Create images of desktops for easy backup and recovery | No | No | Yes | Yes | Yes |
| Windows Shadow Copy (automatically backs up files for easy restore) | No | No | Yes | Yes | Yes |
| Fax and scan | No | No | Yes | Yes | Yes |
| Windows Media Center | No | Yes | No | No | Yes |
| BitLocker Drive Encryption | No | No | No | Yes | Yes |
| Capability to create themed slide shows | No | Yes | No | No | Yes |
| Windows Movie Maker | Yes | Yes | No | No | Yes |
| Wireless network provisioning (allows administrators to set network-side security settings) | No | No | Yes | Yes | Yes |
| Encrypting File System | No | No | Yes | Yes | Yes |

*Table 1-1. Comparing selected features in various versions of Windows Vista (continued)*

| Feature | Home Basic | Home Premium | Business | Enterprise Edition | Ultimate |
|---|---|---|---|---|---|
| Network Access Protection (stops nonsecure PCs from connecting to a network) | No | No | Yes | Yes | Yes |
| Windows Anytime Upgrade (automated online upgrades to Windows Vista) | Yes | Yes | Yes | No | No |
| Network projection (allows connecting to network projectors wirelessly) | No | Yes | Yes | Yes | Yes |
| Windows Meeting Space (allows collaboration over networks) | Can view meetings only | Yes | Yes | Yes | Yes |
| Domain support (allows a PC to join a corporate domain) | No | No | Yes | Yes | Yes |
| Group Policy support (for administrators to set corporate-wide configuration) | No | No | Yes | Yes | Yes |
| Offline files and folders (allows users to automatically sync network files and folders) | No | No | Yes | Yes | Yes |

# Hardware Requirements

Windows Vista requires considerable hardware—significantly more than previous versions of Windows. It needs a lot of graphics horsepower to support the full Aero interface, but it is possible to run Windows Vista without running Aero.

Because there are so many different versions of Windows Vista, and because it is possible to run Windows Vista without the Windows Aero interface, the exact hardware requirements are somewhat confusing. To help make things a little less confusing, Microsoft has set two levels of hardware: Windows Vista Capable and Windows Vista Premium Ready. A Windows Vista Capable PC will not be able to run all of the Windows Vista features, notably Windows Aero.

A Windows Vista Capable PC has these minimum hardware requirements:

- An 800 MHz 32-bit (x86) or 64-bit (x64) processor
- 512 MB of RAM
- DirectX 9-capable graphics processor (Windows Display Driver Model [WDDM] driver support recommended) with a minimum of 64 MB of memory, preferably 128 MB
- 20 GB hard disk, with at least 15 GB free

A Windows Vista Premium Ready PC has these minimum hardware requirements:

- A 1 GHz 32-bit (x86) or 64-bit (x64) processor
- 1 GB of RAM
- DirectX 9-capable graphics processor that supports WDDM driver support, Pixel Shader 2.0, 32 bits per pixel, and a minimum of 128 MB of memory
- 40 GB hard disk, with at least 15 GB free
- DVD-ROM drive

Obviously, more is better, so it's a good idea to exceed these requirements when possible.

# Windows System Performance Rating

Windows Vista includes a performance rating system, which may puzzle you at first. After all, your hardware can clearly support Windows Vista if you're able to run the tool, so what is its purpose?

In fact, it's not designed to tell you how well your PC runs Vista, but rather how well it can run other software. The idea is that software makers will assign their software a certain level, and you'll buy only the software that the performance rating system says you can run. The higher the number is, the better the performance.

In theory, that's fine. But it's not clear how well it will work in practice, because software makers, including Microsoft, have yet to rate their software according to this system. And it's also quite mysterious how the performance rating system calculates its ratings. As you can see in Figure 1-6, the individual components of this PC rate relatively high, from a 5 (the top rating) to a 3.7. So why is the overall system rating a 3.7? Windows Vista automatically takes the lowest component rating and uses that as the overall system rating.

*Figure 1-6. Performance rating*

Useful or not, you might want to see how Windows Vista rates your hardware. Choose Control Panel → System and Maintenance → Performance Information and Tools.

# The Desktop

Like most modern operating systems that use graphical user interfaces or GUIs (such as Mac OS X, Unix, and earlier versions of Windows), Windows Vista uses the metaphor of a Desktop with windows and file folders laid out on it. A program called Windows Explorer (*explorer.exe*) provides this Desktop metaphor.

Figure 1-7 shows the main features of the Windows Vista Desktop. The callouts in the figure highlight some of the special-purpose icons and buttons that may appear.

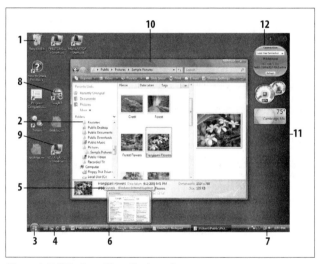

*Figure 1-7. Windows Vista Desktop features*

1. Drag files to the *Recycle Bin* to delete them. Open the bin and rummage through it to recover deleted files.
2. A folder lets you organize your files.
3. The *Start* button gives you access to commands and applications on your system.

4. The *Quick Launch* toolbar gives you fast access to frequently used applications.

5. Hover your mouse over a taskbar window icon, and you will see a live thumbnail of its content.

6. The *Taskbar* contains icons for each running application, plus toolbars and the notification area.

7. The *System Tray* (also called the notification area) contains the clock and useful status indicators about programs and services currently running.

8. A shortcut links to a file, folder, or program somewhere else on the system. You can differentiate between shortcuts and regular icons because shortcuts have a curved arrow on them.

9. You can have shortcuts to other computers on your network.

10. An open folder shows its contents in a window.

11. The *Sidebar* is used to display Gadgets.

12. *Gadgets* are mini-applications that can display changing content, such as stock prices or RSS feeds.

## Point-and-Click Operations

Windows Vista offers several settings that affect the way the interface responds to mouse clicks. The default setting (the way it works when you first install Windows Vista) will also be familiar to most users, as it is consistent with the way most operating systems work.

If you modify certain settings using the Folder Options dialog (Control Panel → Appearance and Personalization → Folder Options), however, Windows may respond differently.

If you are a new computer user who hasn't used a GUI before, here are some things you need to know:

- PCs usually come with a two- or three-button mouse, although there are a variety of alternatives, such as touch-pads (common on laptops), trackballs, and styluses. Many mice also include a scroll wheel which, as its name implies, you use to scroll through pages and screens.

- To *click* an object means to move the pointer to the desired screen object and press and release the left mouse button.

- *Double-click* means to click twice in rapid succession with the button on the left. (Clicking twice slowly doesn't accomplish the same thing.)

- *Right-click* means to click with the button on the right.

- If your pointing device has three or more buttons, you should use just the primary buttons on the left and the right, and read the documentation that comes with your pointing device to find out what you can do with the others. (You can often configure the middle button to take over functions such as double-clicking, cut and paste, inserting inflammatory language into emails, and so on.)

# Windows and Menus

Any open window contains a frame with a series of standard decorations and tools, as shown in Figure 1-8. To move a window from one place to another, click on the title bar and drag. The exact tools and functions available in any window vary according to the application or tool that launches it. Figure 1-8 shows a folder window, which is perhaps the most complicated window in Windows Vista.

Most types of windows are resizable, meaning that you can stretch them horizontally and vertically to make them smaller or larger. Just grab an edge or a corner and start dragging. There are two shortcuts that come in quite handy: maximize and minimize. If you click the maximize button (the middle button in the cluster in the upper right of most windows), the window will be resized to fill the screen. You can't move or resize maximized windows. If you minimize a window (the leftmost button in the cluster), it is shrunk out of sight and appears only as a button on the Taskbar. Minimizing is handy to get windows out of the way without closing them.

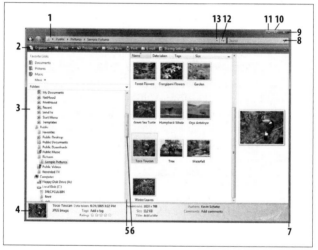

Figure 1-8. The decorations of a standard window: a title bar, title buttons, a menu, and a scrollable client area

1. The *Address Bar* (shows the current folder in Windows Explorer).

2. Application-specific toolbar.

3. *Navigation pane* (Windows Explorer only).

4. *Details pane* (Windows Explorer only). In many applications, this area is taken up by a status bar that gives information about the content of the window.

5. The scroll bar. Click here to move down one line, or scroll by keeping the mouse button depressed.

6. Drag this to jump scroll to a corresponding point in the document.

7. Drag here to resize window.

8. The search bar. It is available in some applications, such as Windows Explorer and Internet Explorer, but not others.

9. Click here to close the window.

10. Click here to maximize the window (make it full screen).

11. Click here to minimize the window (make it into a button on the Taskbar).

12. Refresh the current window. This icon is available in some applications, such as Windows Explorer and Internet Explorer, but not others.

13. Show the history of the current window, such as displaying other folders you've visited recently in Windows Explorer. This icon is available in some applications, such as Windows Explorer and Internet Explorer, but not others.

Under certain circumstances, one or two scroll bars might appear along the bottom and far right of a window. These allow you to move the window's view so that you can see all of its contents. This behavior can be counterintuitive for new users because moving the scroll bar in one direction will cause the window's contents to move in the opposite direction. Look at it this way: the scroll bar doesn't move the contents; it moves the *viewport*. Imagine a very long document with very small type. Moving the scroll bars is like moving a magnifying glass—if you move the glass down the document and look through the magnifier, it looks like the document is moving upward.

If multiple windows are open, only one window has the focus. The window with the focus is usually (but not always) the one on top of all the other windows. The Windows Vista Aero Glass interface features transparent edges to windows, so you will be able to see through the edges of the focused window to windows beneath it. It can be difficult in Windows Vista to know which window has focus if several are side by side, because the Aero Glass interface doesn't necessarily make the border and title of the active windows obviously different from the other windows. The window with the focus is the one that responds to keystrokes, although any window will respond to mouse clicks. To give any window the focus, just click on any visible portion of it, and it will pop to the front. Be careful where you click on the intended window, however, as the click may go further than simply activating it (if you click on a button on a window that doesn't have the focus, for example, it will not only activate the window, but press the button as well).

There are three other ways to activate (assign the focus to) a window. You can click on the Taskbar button that corresponds to the window you want to activate, and it will be brought to the front. If it is minimized (shrunk out of sight), it will be brought back (restored) to its original size. Another way is to use a feature called Windows Flip. Hold down the Alt key and press Tab, and you'll see thumbnails of all your open windows. Keep holding down the Alt key and pressing Tab until you highlight the window you want to open, then release the keys, and you'll be sent to that window. Similarly, to use Windows Flip 3D, hold down the Windows logo key and press Tab, and you'll see thumbnails of all your windows in a 3D stack. Scroll through them by continuing to hold the Windows logo key and pressing Tab until you get to the window you want. Figure 1-9 shows Windows Flip in action, and Figure 1-10 shows Windows Flip 3D.

Just as only one window can have the focus at any given time, only one control (text field, button, checkbox, etc.) can have the focus at any given time. Different controls show focus in different ways: pushbuttons and checkboxes have a dotted rectangle, for instance. A text field (edit box) that has the focus will not be visually distinguished from the rest, but it will be the only one with a blinking text cursor (insertion

*Figure 1-9. Switching among windows using Windows Flip*

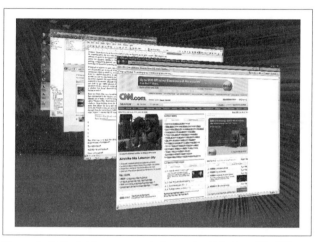

*Figure 1-10. Switching among windows using Windows Flip 3D, which works only if you're using Aero*

point). To assign the focus to a different control, just click on it or use the Tab key (use Shift-Tab to go backward).

Often, new and veteran users are confused and frustrated when they try to type into a window and nothing happens—this is caused by nothing more than the wrong window having the focus. (I've seen skilled touch-typists complete an entire sentence without looking, only to realize that they forgot to click first.) Even if the desired window is in front, the wrong control (or even the menu) may have the focus.

You can configure some windows to be "always on top." This means that they will appear on top of other windows, even if they don't have the focus. Floating toolbars, the Task-bar, and some help screens are common examples. If you have two windows that are "always on top," they behave the same as normal windows, because one can cover the other if it is activated, but both will always appear in their own "layer" on top of all the normal windows.

The Desktop is also a special case. Although it can have the focus, it will never appear on top of any other window. To access something on the Desktop, you have two choices: minimize all open windows by holding the Windows logo key and pressing the D key, or press the Show Desktop button on the Quick Launch Toolbar to temporarily hide all running applications. You can also minimize your current window, although in some instances, that only leads you to the next open window you need to minimize, and so on, until you reach the Desktop.

Many windows have a menu bar, commonly containing standard menu items such as File, Edit, View, and Help, as well as application-specific menus. Click on the menu title to drop it down, and then click on an item in the menu to execute it. Any menu item with a small black arrow that points to the right leads to a secondary, cascading menu with more options. Generally, menus drop down and cascading menus open to the right; if there isn't room, Windows pops them up in the opposite direction. If you want to cancel a menu, simply click anywhere outside of the menu bar.

Those who are used to previous versions of Windows may be somewhat confused by the absence of menus—which have now been replaced by new toolbars—in Internet Explorer and Windows Explorer. New toolbars take the place of menus in them. However, if you're a fan of the old menus, you can still find them; press the Alt or F10 key and they'll magically appear.

Each window also has a Control menu hidden behind the upper-left corner of the title bar (the bar at the top of the window that contains the filename). You can open the menu by clicking on the upper-left corner, by pressing Alt-space, or by right-clicking on a button on the Taskbar. The Control menu duplicates the function of the maximize, minimize, and close buttons at the right end of the title bar, as well as the resizing and moving you can do with the mouse. Using this menu lets you move or resize the window without the mouse. The command line (which you can get to by typing **command** at the Search box and pressing Enter to open a Command Prompt window) also has a Control menu, which you can access by right-clicking anywhere in the Command Prompt window. It provides access to the Clipboard for cut, copy, and paste actions, as well as settings for the font size and toolbar (if applicable). However, if you have enabled the Command Prompt's QuickEdit Mode, right-clicking will paste the contents of the Clipboard into whatever program happens to be running in the Command Prompt.

# Files, Folders, and Disks

Files are the basic unit of long-term storage on a computer. Files are organized into folders, which are stored on disks. (In DOS, Unix, and earlier versions of Windows, folders were more often referred to as *directories*, but both terms are still used.) This section reviews fundamental filesystem concepts, including file- and disk-naming conventions and file types.

## Disk Names

Like every version of Windows that preceded it, Windows Vista retains the basic DOS disk-naming conventions. Drives are differentiated by a single letter of the alphabet followed by a colon:

*A:* Represents the first "floppy" (usually 3.5-inch) disk drive on the system

*B:* Represents the second floppy disk drive, if present

*C:* Represents the first hard disk drive or the first partition of the first hard disk drive

*D:* Often represents a DVD-ROM or CD-ROM drive, but can represent an additional hard disk drive or other removable drive

*E: through Z:*
Represent additional hard disk drives, DVD-ROM or CD-ROM drives, Universal Serial Bus (USB) flash drives, removable cartridges such as ZIP or Jaz drives, or mapped network drives

By default, drive letters are assigned consecutively, but it's possible to change the drive letters for most drives so that you can have a drive *N:* without having a drive *M:*.

## Pathnames

Folders, which contain files, are stored hierarchically on a disk and can be nested to any arbitrary level.

The filesystem on any disk begins with the root (top-level) directory, represented as a backslash. Thus, *C:\* represents the root directory on the *C:* drive. Each additional nested directory is simply listed after its "parent," with backslashes used to separate each one. *C:\Windows\System\Color* means that the Color folder is in the System folder in the Windows folder on the *C:* drive. Thus, you can express a *path* to any given folder as a single string of folder names.

A path can be *absolute* (always starting with a drive letter) or *relative* (referenced with respect to the current directory). The concept of a *current directory* is somewhat obsolete in Windows Vista, as it was in Windows NT, Windows 2000, and Windows XP, with the exception of commands issued from the Command Prompt. Each Command Prompt window has an active folder associated with it, to which each command is directed. For example, if the current directory is *C:\windows*, and you type **DIR** (the directory listing command), you would get a listing of the files in that folder. If you then type **CD cursors**, the current directory would become *C:\windows\cursors*.

The fact that the entire absolute path was not needed after the CD command is an example of the use of a relative path.

A special type of relative path is made up of one or more dots. The names . and .. refer to the current directory and the parent of that directory, respectively (*C:\windows* is the parent folder of *C:\windows\cursors*, for example). Type **CD ..** while in *C:\windows*, and the current directory becomes simply *C:\*. Use of additional dots (such as ...) in some previous versions of Windows is not supported in Windows XP or Vista. The graphical equivalent of .. is the yellow folder icon with the curved arrow, found in common file dialogs.

The left pane (Navigation Pane) in Windows Explorer (by default) contains a hierarchical tree-structured view of the filesystem. The tree structure makes it easier to navigate through all the folders on your system because it provides a graphical overview of the structure.

## Paths to Network Resources

You can refer to files on any shared network via a Universal Naming Convention (UNC) pathname, which is very similar to a path (described in the preceding section). The first element of a UNC pathname is the name of the computer or device that contains the file, prefixed by a double backslash. The second element is the device's share name. What follows is the string of folders leading to the target folder or file.

For example, the UNC path *\\shoebox\o\hemp\adriana.txt* refers to a file named *adriana.txt*, located in the *hemp* folder, located on drive *O:* (which has been shared as *o*), located on a computer named *shoebox*.

---

## Short Names and Long Names

DOS and Windows 3.1, the Microsoft operating systems that preceded Windows 95 and Windows NT, only supported filenames with a maximum of eight characters, plus a three-character file type extension (e.g., *myfile.txt*). The maximum length of any path was 80 characters (see "Pathnames," earlier in this chapter, for more information on paths). Legal characters included any combination of letters and numbers, extended ASCII characters with values greater than 127, and the following punctuation characters:

$ % ^ ' ` - _ @ ~ ! ( ) # &

Spaces were not allowed.

Windows Vista supports long filenames (up to 260 characters), which can include spaces as well as these punctuation characters:

$ % ^ ' ` - _ @ ~ ! ( ) # & + , ; = [ ] .

For example, a file could be named *Picture of my Niece.jpg* and could be located in a folder named *Family Photos*. Furthermore, extensions are no longer limited to three characters; for example, *.html* is perfectly valid (and distinctly different from *.htm*). For more information on file types and extensions, see the discussions in the next section.

The maximum length of any path in Windows Vista depends on the filesystem you're using (NTFS, FAT32, etc.).

## File Types and Extensions

Most files have a filename extension, the (usually three) letters that appear after the last dot in any file's name. Here are some common file extensions:

*.xls*
> An Excel spreadsheet

*.txt*
> A text file (to be opened with Notepad)

*.html*

> A HyperText Markup Language (HTML) file, commonly known as a web page

*.jpg*

> A JPEG image file, used to store photos

Although each of these files holds very different types of data, the only way Windows differentiates them is by their filename extensions. How Windows is able to determine a given file's type is important for several reasons, especially because it is the basis for the associations that link documents with the applications that created them. For example, when you double-click on a file named *donkey.html*, Windows looks up the extension in the Registry and then, by default, opens the file in your web browser. Rename the file to *donkey.jpg*, and the association changes as well.

The lesson here is that filename extensions are not a reliable guide to a file's type, despite how heavily Windows Vista relies on them. What can make it even more frustrating is that, by default, known filename extensions are hidden by Windows Vista, but unfamiliar extensions are shown. Rename *donkey.xyz* (an unassociated extension) to *donkey.txt*, and the extension simply disappears in Windows Explorer. Or, try to differentiate *donkey.txt* from *donkey.doc* when the extensions are hidden. To instruct Windows to show all extensions, go to Control Panel → Appearance and Personalization → Folder Options → View, and turn off the "Hide file extensions for known file types" option.

To see all of the configured file extensions on your system, go to Start → Default Programs → Associate a file type or protocol with a program. You'll see a list of all your file types, along with the programs with which they are associated. To change the default program for any file type, highlight the file type, click "Change program," and then select the new program with which the file should be associated.

# CHAPTER 2

# Shortcuts

There are many different ways to improve your experience with Windows Vista. Some solutions involve making modifications and additions to the operating system, while others describe how to work with the tools that come out of the box. The tips in this chapter illustrate the various keyboard and mouse shortcuts available in Windows Vista.

## Working with Files and Objects

The tips that follow show you how to predict—and even change—how Windows Explorer responds to the dragging and dropping of files and objects. Here's an overview of how drag-and-drop works in Windows Explorer:

- If you drag an object from one place to another on the same physical drive (*c:\docs* to *c:\files*), the object is moved.

- If you drag an object from one physical drive to another physical or network drive (*c:\docs* to *d:\files*), the object is copied, resulting in two identical files on your system.

- If you drag an object from one physical or network drive to another and then back to the first drive, but in a different folder (*c:\docs* to *d:\files* to *c:\stuff*), you'll end up with three copies of the object.

- If you drag an application executable (an EXE file), the same rules apply to it that apply to other objects, except that if you drag it into any portion of your Start menu or into any subfolder of your Start Menu folder, Windows will create a shortcut to the file. Dragging other file types (documents, script files, or other shortcuts) to the Start menu will simply move or copy them there, according to the preceding rules.

- If you drag a system object (such as an item in the My Computer window or the Control Panel) anywhere, a shortcut to the item is created. This, of course, is a consequence of the fact that these objects aren't actually files and can't be duplicated or removed from their original locations.

- If you drag system icons or items that appear within system folders, such as Documents, Internet Explorer, or the Recycle Bin, any number of things can happen, depending on the specific capabilities of the object. For example, if you drag a recently deleted file from the Recycle Bin, it will always be moved, because making a copy of, or a shortcut to, a deleted file makes no sense.

If you have trouble remembering these rules, or if you run into a confusing situation, you can always fall back on the information Windows provides you while you're dragging, in the form of the mouse cursor. A blue right-pointing arrow appears next to the pointer when copying, and a curved arrow appears when creating a shortcut. If you see no symbol, the object will be moved. This visual feedback is very important; it can eliminate a lot of mistakes if you pay attention to it.

Here's how to control what happens when you drag and drop an item:

- To copy an object in any situation, hold the Ctrl key while dragging. Of course, this won't work for system objects such as Control Panel items—a shortcut will be created regardless. Using the Ctrl key in this way will also work when dragging a file from one part of a folder to another part of the same folder, which is an easy way to duplicate a file or folder.

- To move an object in any situation, hold the Shift key while dragging. This also won't work for system objects such as Control Panel items—a shortcut will be created regardless.

- To create a shortcut to an object in any situation, hold the Ctrl and Shift keys simultaneously while dragging. If you try to make a shortcut that points to another shortcut, the shortcut will simply be copied (duplicated).

- To choose what happens to dragged files each time without having to press any keys, drag your files with the right mouse button, and a special menu will appear when the files are dropped. This context menu is especially helpful because it will display only options appropriate to the type of object you're dragging and the place where you've dropped it.

# Starting Up Applications

Windows Vista has more ways to launch a program than just about any other operating system:

- Double-click on a program icon in Explorer, or on the Desktop.

- Double-click on a file associated with an application to launch that application and open the file.

- Pick the name of a program from the Start menu.

- Click on a program's icon in the Quick Launch Toolbar to start it. This toolbar can include icons for any programs, although by default, it often has icons only for Internet Explorer, the Desktop (click it to go to the Desktop), Switch Between Windows, and Windows Mail after you set up Windows Mail the first time.

- Right-click on a file, executable, or application icon and choose Open.

- Select (highlight) an icon and press the Enter key.

---

- Type the filename of a program in the Address Bar, which is displayed above the toolbar in any folder window, in Explorer, in Internet Explorer, or even as part of the Taskbar. You may also have to include the path (the folder and drive names) for some items.

- Type in the filename of a program from the Start Search box and press Enter. You may also have to include the path (the folder and drive names) for some items.

- Type in the first few letters or the entire name of a program (not necessarily the filename) in the Start Search box, choose the program you want to run from the list that appears, and press Enter. For example, if you wanted to run Microsoft Word, you could type **Word**, then select the Microsoft Word icon and press Enter.

- Open a Command Prompt window and type the name of the program at the prompt. Note that some knowledge of the command prompt, which borrows a lot of syntax and commands from Vista's great-grandfather, the Disk Operating System (DOS), is required.

- Create shortcuts to files or applications. A shortcut is a kind of pointer or link—a small file and associated icon that point to a file or program in another location. You can put these shortcuts on the Desktop, in the Start menu, or anywhere else you find convenient. Double-click on a shortcut to launch the program. To launch programs automatically at startup, just place a shortcut in your Startup folder (*C:\Users\username\AppData\Roaming\Microsoft\Windows\Start Menu\Programs\StartUp*).

Some programs are really "in your face." For example, if you install AOL, it often puts an icon on the Desktop, in the Quick Launch Toolbar, and on the All Programs menu, and even shoehorns an icon into the System Tray, which is normally reserved for system status indicators. Other, less obtrusive programs may be more difficult to locate. In fact, you'll probably find several programs mentioned in this book that you never even knew you had!

# Keyboard Shortcuts

This section lists many useful keyboard accelerators. The listings are organized both by keystroke (alphabetically within groups such as function key, Alt-key combination, and so forth) and by function or context (during startup, in the Recycle Bin, for managing windows, and so forth). The first section lists the key and then the function. The second section lists the desired function and then the required key(s).

Note that in addition to the standard keyboard accelerators, you can define accelerators of your own. For example, you can define a Ctrl-Alt combination to invoke any shortcut, whether it's on the Desktop, in the Start menu, or in any other folder. Right-click any Windows shortcut icon (even those right in your Start menu), select Properties, choose the Shortcut tab, and in the Shortcut key field, type the key (not including Ctrl and Alt) to which the shortcut should be linked. For example, to assign Ctrl-Alt-Z to the current shortcut, simply type **Z** in the field. You can use any key except Esc, Enter, Tab, the Space bar, PrintScreen, Backspace, and Delete. If it conflicts with an accelerator used by any existing application, the accelerator you've just defined will usually override the existing accelerator (test it to make sure). To clear an existing shortcut's accelerator, just empty the Shortcut key field on the shortcut's Properties sheet. These instructions apply to Windows shortcuts only. Internet shortcuts don't support keyboard accelerators.

## Keyboard Accelerators Listed by Key

Tables 2-1 through 2-7 list keystrokes that will work in Windows Explorer and most of the components that come with Windows Vista. However, some applications (including Microsoft applications) don't always follow the rules.

---

*Table 2-1. Function keys*

| Key | Action |
| --- | --- |
| F1 | Start Help (supported in most applications). |
| F2 | Rename selected icon or file in Windows Explorer or on the Desktop. |
| F3 | Open Search (in Windows Explorer or on the Desktop only). |
| F4 | Open a drop-down list (supported in many dialog boxes)—for example, press F4 in a File Open dialog to drop down the Look In list. |
| F5 | Refresh the view in Windows Explorer, on the Desktop, in the Registry Editor, and some other applications. |
| F6 | Move focus between panes in Windows Explorer. |
| F10 | Send focus to the current application's menu. |

*Table 2-2. Miscellaneous keys*

| Key | Action |
| --- | --- |
| Arrow keys | Basic navigation: move through menus, reposition the text cursor (insertion point), change the file selection, and so on. |
| Backspace | Move up one level in the folder hierarchy (Windows Explorer only). |
| Delete | Delete selected item(s) or selected text. |
| Down arrow | Open a drop-down listbox. |
| End | Go to end of line when editing text, or to the end of file list. |
| Enter | Activate highlighted choice in menu or dialog box, or insert a carriage return when editing text. |
| Esc | Close dialog box, message window, or menu without activating any choice (usually the same as clicking Cancel). |
| Home | Go to beginning of line (when editing text), or to the beginning of file list. |
| Page down | Scroll down one screen. |
| Page up | Scroll up one screen. |
| PrintScreen | Copy entire screen as a bitmap to the Clipboard. |
| Space bar | Toggle a checkbox that is selected in a dialog box, activate the command button with the focus, or toggle the selection of files when selecting multiple files with Ctrl. |
| Tab | Move focus to next control in a dialog box or window (hold Shift to go backward). |

*Table 2-3. Alt key combinations*

| Key(s) | Action |
| --- | --- |
| Alt (by itself) | Send focus to the menu (same as F10). Also turns on the menu in applications where it is no longer used by default, such as Windows Explorer and Internet Explorer. |
| Alt-*x* | Activate menu or dialog control, where letter *x* is underlined (if the underlines are not visible, pressing Alt will display them). |
| Alt-double-click (on icon) | Display Properties sheet. |
| Alt-Enter | Display Properties sheet for selected icon in Windows Explorer or on the Desktop. Also switches command prompt between windowed and full-screen display. |
| Alt-Esc | Drop active window to bottom of pile, which, in effect, activates next open window. |
| Alt-F4 | Close current window; if Taskbar or Desktop has the focus, exit Windows. |
| Alt-hyphen | Open the current document's system menu in a multiple document interface (MDI) application. |
| Alt-*numbers* | When used with the numbers on the numeric keypad only, inserts special characters corresponding to their ASCII codes into many applications. For example, press the Alt key and type **0169** for the copyright symbol. |
| Alt-PrintScreen | Copy active window as a bitmap to the Clipboard. |
| Alt-Shift-Tab | Same as Alt-Tab, but in the opposite direction. |
| Alt-Space bar | Open the current window's system menu. |
| Alt-Tab | Switch to the next running application—hold Alt while pressing Tab to cycle through running applications. |
| Alt-M | When the Taskbar has the focus, minimize all windows and move focus to the Desktop. |
| Alt-S | When the Taskbar has the focus, open the Start menu. |

*Table 2-4. Ctrl key combinations*

| Keys | Action |
| --- | --- |
| Ctrl-A | Select all; in Windows Explorer, selects all files in the current folder. In word processors, selects all text in the current document. |
| Ctrl-Alt-*x* | User-defined accelerator for a shortcut, in which *x* is any key (discussed at the beginning of this chapter). |
| Ctrl-Alt-Delete | Show the logon dialog when no user is currently logged on; otherwise, switch to the Windows Security dialog, which provides access to Task Manager and Log Off, as well as switching to another user, allowing you to change your password or lock the computer. Use Ctrl-Alt-Delete to access the Task Manager when Explorer crashes or your computer becomes unresponsive. |
| Ctrl-arrow key | Scroll without moving selection. |
| Ctrl-click | Use to select multiple, noncontiguous items in a list or in Windows Explorer. |
| Ctrl-drag | Copy a file. |
| Ctrl-End | Move to the end of a document (in many applications). |
| Ctrl-Esc | Open the Start menu; press Esc and then Tab to move focus to the Taskbar, or press Tab again to move focus to the Taskbar, and then cycle through the toolbars on the Taskbar every time you press Tab. |
| Ctrl-F4 | Close a document window in an MDI application. |
| Ctrl-F6 | Switch between multiple documents in an MDI application. Similar to Ctrl-Tab; hold Shift to go in reverse. |
| Ctrl-Home | Move to the beginning of a document (in many applications). |
| Ctrl-Space bar | Select or deselect multiple, noncontiguous items in a listbox or in Windows Explorer. |
| Ctrl-Tab | Switch among tabs in a tabbed dialog or Internet Explorer; hold Shift to go in reverse. |
| Ctrl-C | Copy the selected item or selected text to the Clipboard. Also interrupts some command prompt applications. |
| Ctrl-F | Open Search (in Windows Explorer or on the Desktop only). |
| Ctrl-V | Paste the contents of the Clipboard. |
| Ctrl-X | Cut the selected item or selected text to the Clipboard. |
| Ctrl-Z | Undo; for example, erases text just entered, and repeals the last file operation in Windows Explorer. |

*Table 2-5. Shift key combinations*

| Key(s) | Action |
|--------|--------|
| Shift | While inserting a CD, hold to disable AutoPlay. |
| Shift-arrow keys | Select text or select multiple items in a listbox or in Windows Explorer. |
| Shift-click | Select all items between currently selected item and item on which you're clicking; also works when selecting text. |
| Shift-click Close button | Close current folder and all parent folders (Windows Explorer in single-folder view only). |
| Shift-Alt-Tab | Same as Alt-Tab, but in reverse. |
| Shift-Ctrl-Tab | Same as Ctrl-Tab, but in reverse. |
| Shift-Ctrl-Esc | Open the Task Manager. |
| Shift-Delete | Delete a file without putting it in the Recycle Bin. |
| Shift-double-click | Open folder in two-pane Explorer view. |
| Shift-Tab | Same as Tab, but in reverse. |

*Table 2-6. Windows logo key (WIN) combinations*

| Key(s) | Action |
|--------|--------|
| WIN | Open the Start menu. |
| WIN-Tab | If the Aero interface is active, this activates Windows Flip 3D. |
| WIN-Pause/Break | Display System Control Panel applet. |
| WIN-Space bar | Display the Sidebar. |
| WIN-D | Minimize all windows and move focus to Desktop. |
| WIN-E | Start Windows Explorer. |
| WIN-F | Launch Search. |
| Ctrl-WIN-F | Search for a computer on your network (requires Active Directory). |
| WIN-L | Lock computer, requiring password to regain access.[a] |
| WIN-M | Minimize current window. |
| Shift-WIN-M | Undo minimize current window. |
| WIN-R | Display Run dialog. |
| WIN-U | Open the Ease of Access Center. |

[a] You can also lock your computer by pressing Ctrl-Alt-Delete and clicking Lock this Computer.

*Table 2-7. Command Prompt keyboard accelerators*

| Key(s) | Action |
|---|---|
| Left/right arrow | Move cursor backward/forward one character. |
| Ctrl + left/right arrow | Move cursor backward/forward one word. |
| Home/End | Move cursor to beginning/end of line. |
| Up/down arrow | Scroll up (and back) through list of stored commands (called the Command Buffer or History). Each press of the up key recalls the previous command and displays it on the command line. |
| Page Up/Down | Recall oldest/most recent command in buffer. |
| Insert | Toggle insert/overtype mode (block cursor implies overtype mode). |
| Esc | Erase current line. |
| F1 | Repeat text typed in preceding line, one character at a time. |
| F2 + *key* | Repeat text typed in preceding line, up to first character matching *key*. |
| F3 | Repeat text typed in preceding line. |
| F5 | Change the template for F1, F2, and F3 (described earlier) so that earlier commands are used as the template; press F5 repeatedly to cycle through the entire command buffer. |
| F6 | Place an end-of-file character (^Z) at current position of command line. |
| F7 | Show all entries in Command Buffer (History). |
| Alt-F7 | Clear all entries in Command Buffer (History). |
| *chars* + F8 | Entering one or more characters *chars* followed by F8 will display the most recent entry in the Command Buffer beginning with *chars*. Pressing F8 again will display the next most recent matching command, and so on. If no characters are specified, F8 simply cycles through existing commands in buffer. |
| F9 + *command#* | Display designated command on command line; use F7 to obtain numbers. |
| Ctrl-C | Interrupt the output of most Command Prompt applications. |

# Keyboard Accelerators Listed by Function

Table 2-8 lists keys that operate in most contexts—in other words, on the Desktop, in the Explorer, and within most applications and dialogs. Functions are listed alphabetically, except where a logical order might make more sense.

Note also that there is essentially a limitless combination of keystrokes that you can use to activate any particular feature in a given application, all of which you can form by combining the various keystrokes listed in this chapter. For example, you can press Alt-F to open an application's File menu, then press P to Print, then press Enter to begin printing. Or press Ctrl-Esc to open the Start menu, Alt-Enter to open the Taskbar and Start Menu Properties, Ctrl-Tab to open the Taskbar tab (if necessary), and Alt-L to lock (or unlock) the Taskbar.

*Table 2-8. Keyboard accelerators listed by function*

| Key(s) | Action |
|---|---|
| Space bar | Checkbox, toggle on or off |
| Ctrl-C | Clipboard, copy |
| Alt-PrintScreen | Clipboard, copy current window as a bitmap |
| PrintScreen | Clipboard, copy entire screen as a bitmap |
| Ctrl-X | Clipboard, cut |
| Ctrl-V | Clipboard, paste |
| Ctrl-F4 | Close current document |
| Alt-F4 | Close current window |
| Esc | Close dialog box, message window, or menu |
| Space bar | Command button, click |
| Shift-F10, or context menu key on some keyboards | Context menu, open |
| Tab (hold Shift to go in reverse) | Controls cycle focus on a dialog box |
| Ctrl-C | Copy selected item or selected text to the Clipboard |

*Table 2-8. Keyboard accelerators listed by function (continued)*

| Key(s) | Action |
|---|---|
| Ctrl-X | Cut selected item or selected text to the Clipboard |
| Windows Logo Key-B, Space bar | Puts you in the notification area (Windows Logo Key-B), then reveals hidden icons (Space bar) |
| Shift-Delete or Shift-drag item to Recycle Bin | Delete a file without putting it in the Recycle Bin |
| Delete | Delete selected item |
| Ctrl-Esc (or Windows Logo Key), then Esc, Tab, Tab, Tab | Desktop, activate |
| Windows Logo Key-D, or click empty portion of Taskbar and press Alt-M | Desktop, activate by minimizing all windows |
| Tab (hold Shift to go in reverse) | Dialog box, cycle through controls |
| Ctrl-Tab (hold Shift to go in reverse) | Dialog box, cycle through tabs |
| Ctrl-F4 | Document, close |
| Ctrl-Home | Document, move to the beginning |
| Ctrl-End | Document, move to the end |
| Ctrl-F6 or Ctrl-Tab | Document, switch between |
| Down Arrow or F4 | Drop-down listbox, open |
| Alt-F4 | Exit an application |
| Ctrl-Esc, then Alt-F4 | Exit Windows |
| Shift-Delete | File, delete without moving to Recycle Bin |
| Windows Logo Key-F (or F3 or Ctrl-F in Windows Explorer or on the Desktop) | File, search |
| Ctrl-Windows Logo Key-F | Find a computer on your network |
| Windows Logo Key-F (or F3 or Ctrl-F in Windows Explorer or on the Desktop) | Find files or folders |
| Tab (hold Shift to go in reverse) | Focus, move among controls on a dialog box |
| Shift-click Close button | Folder, close current and all parents (Windows Explorer in single-folder view only) |
| Right and left arrows | Folder, expand and collapse folders in tree |
| Shift-double-click | Folder, open in two-pane Explorer view |

*Table 2-8. Keyboard accelerators listed by function (continued)*

| Key(s) | Action |
|---|---|
| Windows Logo Key-F (or F3 or Ctrl-F in Windows Explorer or on the Desktop) | Folder, search |
| F1 | Help (in most applications) |
| Down arrow or F4 | Listbox, drop-down |
| Ctrl-click | Listbox, select multiple items |
| Ctrl-Space bar | Listbox, select or deselect items |
| Windows Logo Key-L (or press Ctrl-Alt-Delete and then Space bar) | Lock computer |
| Alt-*x* if menu doesn't have focus, *x* by itself if menu has focus | Menu, activate specific item with letter *x* underlined |
| Arrow keys | Menu, basic navigation |
| Esc | Menu, close |
| F10 or Alt (by itself) | Menu, move focus to |
| Shift-F10, or context menu key on some keyboards | Menu, open context menu |
| Windows Logo Key-D, or click empty portion of Taskbar and press Alt-M | Minimize all windows and move focus to Desktop |
| Windows Logo Key-M (hold Shift to undo) | Minimize current window |
| F6 | Panes, move focus between |
| Backspace | Parent folder, move to (in Windows Explorer) |
| Ctrl-V | Paste the contents of the Clipboard |
| Alt-double-click, or select and then press Alt-Enter | Properties, display for an icon |
| F5 | Refresh (in Windows Explorer, on the Desktop, and some other applications) |
| F2 | Rename selected icon or file in Windows Explorer or on the Desktop |
| Windows Logo Key-R | Run |
| Alt-PrintScreen | Screenshot, copy current window as a bitmap to the Clipboard |
| PrintScreen | Screenshot, copy entire screen as a bitmap to the Clipboard |

*Table 2-8. Keyboard accelerators listed by function (continued)*

| Key(s) | Action |
| --- | --- |
| Page Down | Scroll down one screen |
| Page Up | Scroll up one screen |
| Ctrl-arrow key | Scroll without moving selection |
| Windows Logo Key-F | Search for files or folders |
| F3 or Ctrl-F | Search for files or folders (in Windows Explorer or on the Desktop only) |
| Ctrl-A | Select all |
| Alt-drag file | Shortcut, create |
| Windows Logo Key or Ctrl-Esc | Start menu, open |
| Alt-Tab or Ctrl-Esc (hold Shift to go in reverse) | Switch to next application |
| Ctrl-F6 or Ctrl-Tab (hold Shift to go in reverse) | Switch to next document window |
| Alt-hyphen | System menu, show for current document |
| Alt-Space bar | System menu, show for current window |
| Windows Logo Key-Pause/Break | System Properties, open |
| Ctrl-Tab (hold Shift to go in reverse) | Tabs, switch between tabs |
| Shift-Ctrl-Esc (or press Ctrl-Alt-Delete and click Task Manager) | Task Manager, open |
| Ctrl-Esc, then Alt-Enter | Taskbar and Start Menu Properties, open |
| Windows Logo Key-Tab | Launches Flip 3D |
| Ctrl-Z | Undo |
| Alt-Tab (hold Shift to go in reverse) | Window, activate next |
| Alt-F4 | Window, close |
| Alt-Esc | Window, drop to bottom of pile |
| Windows Logo Key-M (hold Shift to undo) | Window, minimize |
| Windows Logo Key-D (hold Shift to undo) | Window, minimize all |
| Alt-Tab (hold Shift to go in reverse) | Window, switch to |
| Windows Logo Key-E | Windows Explorer, open |
| F6 | Windows Explorer, switch between panes |

# Internet Explorer Hot Keys

Many people like using the mouse, but those who are more keyboard oriented are always looking for fast ways to access Internet Explorer features. That's where hot key combinations come in; rather than having to mouse around, you can press a simple key combination, such as Ctrl-D, to add a site to your Favorites. Table 2-9 lists Internet Explorer hot keys.

*Table 2-9. Internet Explorer hot keys*

| Key combination | Action |
| --- | --- |
| Alt-left arrow | Go to the preceding page. |
| Alt-right arrow | Go to the next page. |
| Ctrl-Tab/Shift-Ctrl-Tab | Go to the next/previous tab. |
| Escape (Esc) | Stop the page from loading. |
| F5 or Ctrl-F5 | Refresh the page. |
| Alt-Home | Go to your home page. |
| Alt-D | Give focus to the Address Bar. |
| Ctrl-Enter | Add "www." and ".com" to what you typed in the Address Bar, then navigate to the site. |
| Space bar/Shift-Space bar | Scroll down/up the web page. |
| Alt-F4 | Close Internet Explorer. |
| Alt-M | Activate the Home button on the Command Bar. |
| Alt-J | Activate the Feeds button on the Command Bar. |
| Alt-O | Activate the Tools button on the Command Bar. |
| Alt-L | Activate the Help button on the Command Bar. |
| Alt-C | Open the Favorites Center set to display favorites. |
| Ctrl-Shift-Q | Bring up a list of open tabs. |
| Ctrl-D | Add sites to Favorites. |
| Shift-click | Open a link in a new window. |
| Shift-F10 | Open the right-click context menu for the currently selected item. |

*Table 2-9. Internet Explorer hot keys (continued)*

| Key combination | Action |
|---|---|
| Ctrl-mouse wheel up/down | Zoom in/out by 10 percent. |
| Ctrl-(+) | Increase zoom by 10 percent. |
| Ctrl-(−) | Decrease zoom by 10 percent. |
| Ctrl-0 (zero) | Go back to the original size. |
| Ctrl-E | Go to the Toolbar Search Box. |
| Alt-Enter | Open your search query in a new tab. |
| Ctrl-down arrow | Display the search provider menu. |
| Ctrl-I | Open the Favorites Center to your favorites. |
| Ctrl-H | Open the Favorites Center to your history. |
| Ctrl-J | Open the Favorites Center to your feeds. |

# Windows Mail Hot Keys

Many people like using the mouse, but those who are more keyboard-oriented are always looking for fast ways to access Windows Mail features. That's where hot key combinations come in; rather than having to mouse around, you can press a simple key combination. Table 2-10 lists Windows Mail hot keys.

*Table 2-10. Windows Mail keyboard shortcuts*

| Key combination | Action |
|---|---|
| **In Main window, View Message window, and Send Message window** | |
| F1 | Open Help. |
| Ctrl-A | Select all messages or all text within a single message. |
| **In Main window and View Message window** | |
| Ctrl-M | Send and receive email. |
| Ctrl-N | Open or post a new message. |
| Ctrl-Shift-B | Open Contacts. |

*Table 2-10. Windows Mail keyboard shortcuts (continued)*

| Key combination | Action |
|---|---|
| Delete or Ctrl-D | Delete an email message. |
| Ctrl-R | Reply to the message author. |
| Ctrl-Shift-R or Ctrl-G (newsgroups only) | Reply to all. |
| Ctrl-F | Forward a message. |
| Ctrl-Shift-F | Find a message. |
| Ctrl-P | Print the selected message. |
| Ctrl-> | Go to the next message in the list. |
| Ctrl-< | Go to the preceding message in the list. |
| Alt-Enter | View the selected message's properties. |
| Ctrl-U | Go to the next unread email message. |
| Ctrl-Shift-U | Go to the next unread newsgroup conversation. |
| **In Main window** | |
| Ctrl-O or Enter | Open a selected message. |
| Ctrl-Enter or Ctrl-Q | Mark a message as read. |
| Tab | Move among the message list, Folders list (if on), and Preview pane. |
| Ctrl-W | Go to a newsgroup. |
| Left arrow or plus sign (+) | Expand a newsgroup conversation (show all responses). |
| Right arrow or minus sign (−) | Collapse a newsgroup conversation (hide responses). |
| Ctrl-Shift-A | Mark all newsgroup messages as read. |
| Ctrl-J | Go to the next unread newsgroup or folder. |
| Ctrl-Shift-M | Download newsgroup messages for offline reading. |
| Ctrl-I | Go to your Inbox. |
| Ctrl-Y | Go to a folder. |
| F5 | Refresh newsgroup messages and headers. |

*Table 2-10. Windows Mail keyboard shortcuts (continued)*

| Key combination | Action |
| --- | --- |
| **In Message window: viewing or sending** | |
| Esc | Close a message. |
| F3 or Ctrl-Shift-F | Find text. |
| **In Message window: sending only** | |
| F7 | Check spelling. |
| Ctrl-Shift-S | Insert a signature. |
| Ctrl-Enter or Alt-S | Send a message or post it to a newsgroup. |
| Ctrl-Tab | Switch among the Edit, Source, and Preview tabs when working in Source Edit view. |

# CHAPTER 3

# Windows Components, Features, and Settings

This chapter provides a listing of the most useful components, features, and settings that make up Windows Vista—an encyclopedia, if you will, of everything you can do with Windows out of the box. Some of the more prominent applications and utilities that come with Windows Vista are available through shortcuts on the Start menu, but many useful tools aren't as conspicuous, available only to those users who know where to look.

In Windows, there is usually more than one way to accomplish any task. So, each entry in this chapter starts with the format name of the component as it appears on the screen and the executable filename, which can be typed into the address bar, the command prompt, or the Start Search box. Then, its location in the interface (if applicable) is shown with standard path notation, followed by a description, tips, command-line options, or other applicable helpful information.

## The User Interface

### Address Bar

The Address Bar is a special toolbar with an input field and (optionally) an arrow. It appears in Internet Explorer, Windows Explorer, and, if you've right-clicked on the Taskbar and selected Address from the Toolbars menu, on the Taskbar. When you type an Internet address, the name of a program, or the path of a folder, and then press Enter, the Address Bar will respond in one of many ways, depending on its location and your system's settings.

## Bread Crumbs

Windows Explorer now includes bread crumb navigation along the top, which shows you the complete path to your current location. Click on any spot back along the path, and you'll navigate directly there. Click the arrow next to any spot on the path, and you'll see a drop-down list of all the subfolders under that location.

## Change Your Color Scheme

Change the color and "glassiness" of windows, the Start menu, and the Taskbar.

### To open

Control Panel → [Appearance and Personalization] → Personalization → Window Color and Appearance

Right-click the Desktop and choose Personalize → Window Color and Appearance

### Description

One of the most notable changes in Windows Vista compared to earlier versions of Windows is its transparent windows, courtesy of Windows Aero. You can change their colors and transparency from the Window Color and Appearance page.

Click a color to choose a new color. If you want to further customize the colors, click "Show color mixer," and controls will let you choose the precise colors of your windows. To change the transparency of windows, use the Color intensity slider. Move the slider to the left to make windows more transparent and to the right to make them less transparent. To change the colors and fonts of all screen elements in pretty much any way you'd like, click "Open classic appearance properties for more color options," and you'll open a dialog box from Windows Vista that lets you customize all elements of your screen.

---

### TIP

If you aren't using Windows Aero, choosing Window Color and Appearance leads you to a different screen—Appearance Settings, a holdover from Windows XP that lets you choose a color scheme but doesn't let you set the transparency of windows.

---

## Control Panel                                    \windows\system32\control.exe

The central interface for most of the preferences, hardware configurations, and other settings in Windows Vista.

### To open

Start → Control Panel

Windows Explorer → navigate to the *Desktop\Control Panel* folder (it's not available in the *\Users\username\Desktop* folder, however)

Search box or Command Prompt → **Control**

Search box or Command Prompt → **filename.cpl**

### Usage

```
control [filename.cpl] [applet_name]
control [keyword]
filename.cpl
```

### Description

The Control Panel has no settings of its own; it's merely a container for any number of option windows (commonly called applets or *Control Panel extensions*), most of which you can access without even opening the Control Panel folder. Unfortunately, the Control Panel can look vastly different from one computer to another, based on preferences scattered throughout several dialog boxes. Furthermore, the default settings vary, depending on how Windows Vista was installed. To simplify notation in this book, I'm making certain

---

assumptions about your preferences. It's best to familiarize yourself with the various options described here so that you won't be confused when a setting in the Control Panel is referenced.

The Control Panel has two views: the normal view and the "Classic" view. In the normal view, you see major categories and click through to subcategories until you find the setting or applet you're looking for. Windows Vista changes Control Panel behavior to a certain extent compared to Windows XP, because even at the category level, there are applets you can click without having to drill down. The Classic view, by way of contrast, presents a simple, alphabetical listing of all Control Panel applets. To switch from the normal view to the Classic view, click the Classic View link. To switch from the Classic View to the normal view, click Control Panel Home.

See Table 3-1 for a list of Control Panel applets that you can run directly from the command line, and the category in which you can find them. Not listed are applets that you cannot run from the command line.

*Table 3-1. Control Panel applets*

| Applet name | Category | What to type at the command line |
|---|---|---|
| Add Hardware | N/A | `control hdwwiz.cpl` |
| Add or Remove Programs | Programs | `control appwiz.cpl` |
| Administrative Tools | System and Maintenance | `control admintools` |
| Appearance Settings | Appearance and Personalization | `control color` |
| Audio Devices and Sound Themes | Hardware and Sound | `control mmsys.cpl` |
| Date and Time | Clock, Language, and Regions | `control timedate.cpl` or `control date/time` |
| Display Settings | Appearance and Personalization | `control desk.cpl` or `control desktop` |
| Firewall | Security | `control firewall.cpl` |

*Table 3-1. Control Panel applets (continued)*

| Applet name | Category | What to type at the command line |
|---|---|---|
| Folder Options | Appearance and Personalization | control folders |
| Fonts | Appearance and Personalization | Explorer "\windows\fonts"<br>or<br>control fonts |
| Game Controllers | Hardware and Sound | control joy.cpl |
| Infocard | N/A | control infocardcpl.cpl |
| iSCSI Initiator | N/A | control iscsicpl.cpl |
| Internet Options | Network and Internet | control inetcpl.cpl |
| Keyboard | Hardware and Sound | control main.cpl Keyboard<br>or<br>control keyboard |
| Mouse | Hardware and Sound | control main.cpl<br>or<br>control mouse |
| Network Connections | Network and Internet | control ncpa.cpl<br>or<br>control netconnections |
| Pen and Input Devices | Hardware and Sound | control tabletpc.pcl |
| People Near Me | Network and Internet | control collab.pcl |
| Phone and Modem Options | Printers and Other Hardware | control telephon.cpl<br>or<br>control telephony |
| Power Options | Hardware and Sound | control powercfg.cpl |
| Printers and Faxes | Hardware and Sound | control printers |
| Regional and Language Options | Clock, Language, and Regions | control intl.cpl<br>or<br>control international |
| Scanners and Cameras | Hardware and Sound | control sticpl.cpl |

*Table 3-1. Control Panel applets (continued)*

| Applet name | Category | What to type at the command line |
|---|---|---|
| Windows Security Center | Security | `control wscui.cpl` |
| Task Scheduler | System and Maintenance | `control schedtasks` |
| Text to Speech | Ease of Access | `control speech` |
| System | System and Maintenance | `control sysdm.cpl` |
| User Accounts | User Accounts and Family Safety | `control nusrmgr.cpl`<br>or<br>`control userpasswords`<br>or<br>`control userpasswords2` |

## Date and Time Properties

*\windows\system\timedate.cpl*

Set your system's clock, choose a time zone, and enable Internet time synchronization.

### To open

Control Panel → [Clock, Language, and Region] → Date and Time

Right-click on the time in the notification area, and select Adjust Date/Time.

Command Prompt → **timedate.cpl**

Command Prompt → **control date/time**

### Description

The Date and Time dialog is pretty straightforward. Set your system's clock and time zone with the Date and Time tab, add additional clocks with the Additional Clocks tab, and automatically synchronize your PC clock to the true time over the Internet with the Internet Time tab.

Hover your mouse over the time, and the time of your additional clocks pops up in a small display. Click the time for a fuller display.

## Display Settings

Change the settings for your monitor and screen.

### To open

Control Panel → [Appearance and Personalization] → Personalization → Display Settings

Command Prompt → `control desk.cpl`

### Description

Display Settings allows you to change your display hardware settings. Here, you can choose the resolution and color depth of your screen.

## Ease of Access Center

Make it easier to access your computer.

### To open

Control Panel → [Appearance and Personalization] → Ease of Access Center

### Description

If you have problems with your vision, or other issues that make it difficult to interact with your computer, the Control Panel's Ease of Access Center will let you change your settings to make it easier to use your PC.

The center offers these settings. Select any of them, and they will automatically be turned on when you boot up your PC:

*Start Magnifier*
> Lets you enlarge sections of the screen so they're easier to see

*Start On-Screen Keyboard*
> Lets you use a mouse or other pointing device to type by clicking on keys on an on-screen keyboard

*Start Narrator*
> Turns on the Narrator, which reads text aloud from the screen

*Set Up High Contrast*
> Turns on extremely high contrast to reduce eyestrain and make the screen easier to see

---

## Font Viewer

\windows\system32\fontview.exe

Display a preview and summary of any supported font file.

### To open

Control Panel → [Appearance and Personalization] → Fonts → Double-click any font file

### Usage

```
fontview [/p] filename
```

### Description

It's easiest to use Font Viewer by double-clicking on a font file. You can view any font formats normally supported by Windows Vista, including TrueType fonts (*.ttf*), bitmap fonts (*.fon*), and Type 1 fonts (*.pfm*).

In addition to the font name and summary information displayed at the top of the report, a preview of the font is shown with the full alphabet in upper- and lowercase, the full set of numbers, a few symbols, and the phrase "the quick brown fox jumps over the lazy dog. 1234567890" in several different sizes.

---

## Fonts Folder

Display all the installed fonts.

### To open

Control Panel → [Appearance and Personalization] → Fonts

Command Prompt → **control fonts**

Command Prompt → **explorer \windows\fonts**

---

### Description

The Fonts folder is merely a folder on your hard disk (specifically, \*Windows\fonts*). However, when viewed in Explorer, it's configured to display a list of installed fonts instead of a list of the folder's contents. (The two aren't necessarily the same thing.) Select View → Details for a view that lets you match up a font name with the file in which it's stored. Use the Preview Pane for a preview of the font.

## Live Taskbar Thumbnails

This feature of Windows Aero displays a thumbnail of the contents of any window on the Taskbar when the mouse hovers over the window. Above the thumbnail is the name of the application and open file. The thumbnail is actually live; it shows what is currently happening in that window, unless the window is currently minimized. So if a video is playing, you'll see the video playing in the thumbnail. Live Taskbar thumbnails work only when your PC uses Windows Aero.

## Notification Area

The notification area, commonly known as the *Tray*, is the small area at the far right (or bottom) of the Taskbar that, by default, holds the clock and the tiny, yellow speaker icon, among other possible icons. With the exception of the clock, the purpose of the tray is to hold status icons placed there by Windows and other running applications. Hold the mouse cursor over the clock to see the date temporarily or click it to see a full clock. Right-click on an empty area of the Taskbar and click Properties to turn the clock on or off and to change other settings.

## Personalization

Personalize Windows Vista's appearance.

### To open

Control Panel → [Appearance and Personalization] → Personalization

Command Prompt → **control desktop**

---

## Description

This Control Panel category serves as the central location for customizing the way your Desktop and Windows Vista look and sound, and it contains a variety of applets that let you change everything from your desktop background to your display settings, font size, and more.

## Recycle Bin

In the early days of computing, once you deleted a file it was gone. An unerase tool (available as part of Norton Utilities) was commonly used to recover accidentally deleted files. Microsoft caught on, and a while back gave Windows its own Recycle Bin—a feature that gives nearly every file a second chance, so to speak.

Drag any item from the Desktop to the Recycle Bin icon to delete it. When you drag the item and hold it over the Recycle Bin, an arrow appears next to the item. Drop it in the bin and the item disappears. Selecting File → Delete on the menu bar of a folder also moves items to the Recycle Bin, as does selecting the item and then pressing the Delete key. By default, files are not deleted immediately but are stored until the Recycle Bin runs out of space, at which point they are deleted, oldest first, to make space. Until that time, you can retrieve them by double-clicking on the Recycle Bin icon, browsing through the contents of the Recycle Bin window, and dragging or sending the file elsewhere.

## Regional and Language Options                \windows\system32\intl.cpl

Language and localization settings affecting the display of numbers, currency, times, and dates.

### To open

Control Panel → [Clock, Language, and Region] → Regional and Language Options

Command Prompt → `intl.cpl`

Command Prompt → `control international`

## Description

Numbers, times, dates, and currency are displayed differently in different parts of the world, and the Regional and Language Options dialog allows you to choose your display preferences in painful detail.

## Start Menu

The central location for your application shortcuts and many Windows features.

### To open

Desktop → Start

Press the Windows logo key, if you've got one.

Ctrl-Esc

### Description

The Start menu was one of Microsoft's answers to the growing size and complexity of the Windows operating system when it was introduced in Windows 95. Since then, other features have been introduced to compensate for the Start menu's inadequacies, such as the Quick Launch Toolbar, the new Windows Vista-style Start menu, and the new Start Search input box.

---

### TIP

One of the subtler changes to the Start menu is that when you're using Aero Glass, the menu is slightly transparent (translucent, really) so that you can see the content underneath it in a hazy kind of way.

---

Here is a quick rundown of the items you'll find in the Start menu. Note that some of these items may be hidden as a result of changing the Start Menu settings.

*All Programs*

While the Desktop is commonly used to hold icons for the most frequently used programs, the All Programs menu is designed to hold icons for every program installed on your computer. Hold your mouse over the arrow or click it to see a list of all the programs installed on your PC. Some programs are listed directly on the All Programs menu when you click it, and others are organized in folders (Games, Microsoft Office, etc.). The Windows Vista All Programs menu differs significantly from the Windows XP All Programs menu. The Windows XP All Programs menu cascaded; the Windows Vista All Programs menu shows the programs directly on the Start menu itself.

---

### TIP

You can drag and drop programs to any location on the All Programs menu, including inside folders, to change the location where it appears. When you do this, you're not moving the actual program itself, but instead a shortcut to the program.

---

*All Programs → Startup*

To have a program run automatically when Windows starts, place a shortcut to the program in this special folder. If you have more than one user set up on your computer, you'll want to control whether the program starts up automatically for just you or for all users, so instead of dropping it right in your Start menu, right-click on the Start button, choose Open All Users or Explore All Users, click Programs, and then click Startup. From this folder, you can add or delete shortcuts for startup programs.

*Recently Used Programs*

Located just above All Programs, this is a list of the programs you've most recently used. Click any icon to run the program. For security reasons, you may want to disable this menu. To do so, right-click on the Taskbar and choose Properties → Start Menu, uncheck the box next to "Store and display a list of recently opened programs," and then click OK.

*Internet, Email*

These two items are user-customizable links to your favorite web browser and email program, respectively. By default, they're set to Internet Explorer and Windows Mail, but you can replace them with any programs properly registered as web browsers and email clients.

---

### User Account

At the top of the Start menu is your user account icon. Click it to manage your user account. Clicking this icon brings you to the same Control Panel applet as if you followed the path Control Panel → User Accounts and Family Safety → User Accounts.

---

#### TIP

For advanced options for controlling user accounts, at a command prompt type **control userpasswords2**, and use the resulting dialog box.

---

### *username* Button

Just below the User Account icon is a button which, when clicked, opens Windows Explorer to the *username* folder, which contains personal documents, Desktop settings, Favorites, and personal information for the currently logged-on user.

### Documents, Pictures, Music

Clicking any of these buttons brings you to the corresponding folders for the current user account—*username\ Documents*, *username\Pictures*, and *username\Music*.

### Games

This button leads you to the Games folder, which has a list of installed games. It's the same list you'll find if you choose All Programs → Games.

### Search

This brings you to Search.

### Recent Items

This is a list of automatically generated links to the last dozen or so documents that were opened. Click the links to open the documents in their default applications. For security reasons, you may want to disable this menu. To do so, right-click on the Taskbar and choose Properties → Start Menu, uncheck the box next to "Store and display a list of recently opened files," and then click OK.

---

*Favorites*

 This is a mirror of the current user's Favorites folder (*\Users\ username\Favorites*) and the All Users' Favorites folder (*\Users\ All Users\Favorites*). Although this is the same menu you'll see in Windows Explorer and Internet Explorer, the shortcuts in this menu will launch whatever browser is currently registered as the default. By default, this menu is not displayed. To turn it on, right-click on the Taskbar and choose Properties → Start Menu, click Customize, check the box next to "Favorites menu," and click OK.

---

**TIP**

If you're a fan of the Run box from Windows XP, you can have it displayed on the Start menu. Right-click on the Taskbar and choose Properties → Start Menu, click Customize, check the box next to "Run command," and click OK. As a practical matter, there's no real need for this box, though, because the Start Search box does everything that Run does, and more.

---

*Shut Down*

 This lets you shut down your PC, hibernate or sleep it, restart it, switch to another user, and similar options.

*Log Off*

 This logs you off but doesn't shut down your PC.

*Start Search*

 This lets you do a quick search for files, folders, programs, and sites you've visited.

*Computer*

 This opens Windows Explorer to the Computer view of your PC, the topmost level of Windows Explorer, and displays all of your drives.

*Network*

 This opens your network in a Windows Explorer window.

*Connect To*

 This opens the Connect to a Network dialog box, which lets you connect to wireless, dial-up, and VPN networks.

*Control Panel*
> See "Control Panel," earlier in this chapter.

*Default Programs*
> Opens the Default Programs Control Panel applet, which lets you change a variety of settings related to how you run programs in Windows Vista, such as choosing your default programs for email, browsing the Web, and playing music. You can get to this applet via the Control Panel by going to Control Panel → Programs → Default Programs.

*Help and Support*
> This opens the Windows Help and Support Center, where you can search for help, launch troubleshooters, and get help online.

## Taskbar

The Taskbar contains the Start Menu button, buttons representing all open application windows, the notification area (also known as the Tray, discussed earlier in this chapter), and any optional toolbars.

The Start button isn't terribly complicated: just click on it to open the Start menu (discussed earlier in this chapter).

## Windows Aero

Windows Aero (sometimes referred to as *Aero Glass*) represents a significant change in the Windows interface. It adds a variety of new features, including transparent windows, live Taskbar thumbnails, and Windows Flip and Windows Flip 3D, some of which are designed to make it easier to navigate and find useful information (live Taskbar thumbnails and Windows Flip 3D) and others that are designed to make the overall experience more visually pleasing (transparent windows and animation).

## Windows Flip and Windows Flip 3D

Preview open windows and switch among them.

**To open**

Alt → Tab (Windows Flip)

Windows logo key → Tab (Windows Flip 3D)

Click the Windows Flip 3D icon in the Quick Launch area

**Description**

The old Alt-Tab method of switching among windows in Windows XP has been replaced by the far more useful Windows Flip and Windows Flip 3D in Windows Vista. They each let you see thumbnails of your windows before you switch among them, making it easier to decide which window you want to switch to. Windows Flip shows the thumbnails side by side, and Windows Flip 3D shows the thumbnails stacked in three dimensions.

## Windows Sidebar and Gadgets

Gadgets perform automated tasks and display information; they live in the Windows Sidebar on the Desktop.

**To open**

Double-click the Windows Sidebar icon in the notification area.

Control Panel → [Appearance and Personalization] → Windows Sidebar Properties → Start Sidebar when Windows starts

Start → All Programs → Accessories → Windows Sidebar

**Description**

One of Windows Vista's most useful new features is the Windows Sidebar and the Gadgets that live there. Gadgets are mini-applications that automatically perform a variety of useful tasks or display helpful information; many of them are designed to connect to the Internet in order to grab information for you. For example, they can fetch and display current stock information, news, and traffic reports. They can also play live slideshows of pictures on your PC and display information about how your system is currently performing. And they can integrate with your applications to give you a quick way to interact with them, for example, by displaying Really Simple Syndication (RSS) feeds from Internet Explorer, or displaying recent emails.

# Filesystem, Drives, Data, and Search

## File Properties

View and change the properties of files.

### To open

Right-click a file → Properties

Click a file → Organize → Properties

### Description

The File Properties window has four tabs:

*General*
> This tab displays basic information about the file, including
> its location, type, size, and size on disk; the date it was
> created, modified, and last accessed; and its attributes. You
> can change the program that opens it by clicking the Change
> button, and you can change the file attributes by selecting
> Read-only or Hidden. The Advanced button lets you
> compress and/or encrypt the file, add or take away the file
> from the index for searching, and add or take away the
> Archive bit (for use in backups).

---

**TIP**

Why are there two listings for file size—one for size, and
one for size on disk? There are two cases where the file
size and size on disk are different:

- The *cluster size* of your NTFS filesystem dictates the
  size of the chunks that are set aside for files. On an
  NTFS filesystem with 4 KB clusters, a 1 KB file would
  use up 4 KB of disk space, and a 5 KB file would use
  up 8 KB.

- If a file has been compressed, the size listing shows
  its uncompressed size, and the size on disk shows its
  actual size on your hard disk.

---

*Security*

> This tab shows you who has access to read and modify the file
> and its attributes, and lets you change those permissions.
> Click each group and username and you'll be shown the
> rights that person or group has to the file—whether they can
> read the file, modify the file, and so on. You can modify the
> permissions for each person or group, add new groups or
> people and set their permissions, and delete people or groups,
> which means they would have no access to the file.

---

**TIP**

The various file permission options and their meanings
are quite complex, and beyond the scope of this book.
However, if you want more details about the available options, go to the Microsoft Knowledge Base article at *http://
support.microsoft.com/kb/308419/en-us.*

---

*Details*

> This tab displays the metatags associated with the file, as well
> as a wide variety of other information, including the basic file
> information shown in the General tab. It also has a great deal
> of program-specific information. For example, a Word docu-
> ment will display what template was used to create the file,
> the number of pages in the file, the word count, the character
> count, the line count, the paragraph count, the total length of
> time during which the file has been edited, and so on. You
> can also remove metatags and properties from the file by
> clicking the Remove Properties and Personal Information link.
> The details for each file type are quite different from one
> another. Graphics files, for example, include resolution, bit
> depth, width and height, and other similar information, as
> well as a quality rating that users can apply to the file.

*Previous Versions*

> This tab lets you view, save, or restore a previous version of a
> file, if such a version is available. Two types of previous
> versions may be available: those from a backup and those
> from what Windows Vista calls *shadow copies*. A shadow
> copy is a copy of a file made when Windows creates a restore

point. Different files and types of folders have differing options for how you handle previous versions, but in general, you'll be able to open and save the previous version of a file to a different location, or restore it over the existing files.

## Folder Properties

View and change the properties of folders.

### To open

Right-click a folder → Properties

Click a folder → Organize → Properties

### Description

The Folder Properties window has five tabs:

*General*

> This tab displays basic information about the folder, including its parent folder, size, size on disk, date and time created, and number of files and subfolders contained within. The Advanced button lets you compress and/or encrypt the folder, add or take away the folder from the index for searching, and add or take away the Archive bit (for use in backups).

---

**TIP**

Why are there two listings for folder size—one for size, and one for size on disk? If a folder has been compressed, the size listing shows its uncompressed size, and the size on disk shows its actual size on your hard disk.

---

*Sharing*

> This tab lets you set sharing options for the folder. Click Share to share the folder, or change sharing options if the folder is already shared. Click Advanced Sharing if you want to give it a shared name in addition to its existing folder name. You would do this if you wanted to make it easier for someone to find the folder.

---

*Security*

 This tab shows you who has access to read and modify the folder and its attributes, and lets you change those permissions. Click each group and username and you'll be shown the rights that person or group has to the folder—whether they can read it, modify it, and so on. You can modify the permissions for each person or group, add new groups or people and set their permissions, and delete people or groups, which means they would have no access to the folder. The Advanced button gives you additional ways to edit permissions, as well as a way to change who has ownership of the folder.

---

### TIP

The various file permission options and their meanings are quite complex, and beyond the scope of this book. However, if you want more details about the available options, go to the Microsoft Knowledge Base article at *http://support.microsoft.com/kb/308419/en-us*.

---

*Previous Versions*

 This tab lets you view, save, or restore a previous version of a folder, if such a version is available. Two types of previous versions may be available: those from a backup and those from what Windows Vista calls shadow copies. As explained earlier, a shadow copy of a folder is a copy of a file made when Windows creates a restore point. Different files and types of folders have differing options for how you handle previous versions, but in general, you'll be able to open and save the previous version of the folder to a different location, or restore it over the existing folder.

*Customize*

 This tab lets you customize how the folder looks and acts. You can choose the kind of folder it is (All Items, Documents, Pictures and Videos, Music Details, or Music Icons). Based on what type of folder it is, the documents in it will be displayed differently, and different features will be available. For example, if a folder is a Pictures and Videos folder, the details it will display about each file include the date taken, tags, size, and rating, and the folder toolbar will include a Slide Show button so that you can display a slide show of the files in the folder. If the folder is a Documents folder, the details it will display are the date modified, type, size, and tags, but no Slide Show button will appear on the toolbar.

The tab also lets you choose a file that will be displayed on the folder's icon in Windows Explorer, and lets you choose a different icon than the default.

## Indexing Options

Configure and customize the index for searching.

### To open

Control Panel → [System and Maintenance] → Indexing Options

Windows Explorer → Search Tools → Modify Index Locations (the Search Tools icon appears when you type text into the Search box, but it is otherwise invisible)

### Description

The Indexing Options screen shows you what folders are included in your index and lets you add or remove folders. The index is used to speed up searches in Windows Vista.

## Search

Search for files.

### To open

Start → Search

Start → Enter text in Start Search

Enter text in Search box in Windows Explorer.

### Description

Search has been embedded so deeply into Windows Vista and Windows Explorer that at first it can be difficult to know where to begin. Should you use the Search box inside Windows Explorer? The one inside Internet Explorer? The Start Search box that appears when you click the Start button? How about choosing Start → Search to go straight to the Search Folder and Advanced Search screen?

Table 3-2 shows the major ways you can perform a search in Windows Vista and recommendations on when to use which.

*Table 3-2. Different ways to search*

| Search method | When to use it |
| --- | --- |
| Search box in Windows Explorer | Best for searching inside individual folders and subfolders, because it searches only the current folder and subfolders. Also best for searching on filenames. |
| Start → Search (leads to Search folder and Advanced Search) | Best for performing complex searches across multiple folders and for when you want to save a search for future use. |
| Start Search box on the Start menu | Best for quick searches across multiple folders or for searching the Internet. Not good for searching for filenames. |
| Search box in Internet Explorer | Best for searching the Internet. |

Windows Vista performs a search while you type your search term into a Search box. So as you type the letters *vis*, for example, it will display all files that have *vis* in them and will narrow the search as you type more letters into the box.

### Understanding searching and the index

When you search for a file on your computer, you aren't actually searching your entire hard disk. Instead, you're searching the Windows Vista index, which makes searching lightning fast.

---

**TIP**

Sometimes you will search outside the index. For example, when you perform a search inside a folder, you also search the filenames inside the folder, not just the index. And, as explained later, you can also expand your search to nonindexed locations when you want.

---

Although the index makes searching lightning fast, it can cause some confusion, as well. By default, your entire PC is not indexed, because doing that would defeat the purpose of the index—it would get so large that it would slow down your search.

By default, the following are indexed:

- Your user folder (\Users\username), which contains your Documents, Music, Pictures, and Videos folders, as well as Contacts, Favorites, and the hidden AppData folder, which contains your Windows Mail messages.

- Offline files, which are files stored on a server or network drive that you have configured to be available offline.

- The contents of your Start menu.

That's well and good, but what happens if you don't store files and folders underneath your user folder? What if you store them in other places on your hard disk? Then you won't find them when you perform a search, unless you specifically search for them outside the index, which of course defeats the purpose of the index.

There is a solution, however. You can add any folders you want to the index (and take them away, as well). For details, see "Indexing Options," earlier in this chapter. A simple way to get to the Indexing Options screen is from Windows Explorer, by choosing Search Tools → Modify Index Locations. (The Search Tools icon appears only after you type text into the Search box.)

## Windows Explorer                          \windows\explorer.exe

The default Windows interface, including the Start menu, the Desktop, the Taskbar, the Search tool, the Windows Explorer window, and all folder windows.

### To open

Start → All Programs → Accessories → Windows Explorer

Command Prompt → `explorer`

Double-click any folder icon on the Desktop or in any folder window.

Windows Key-E

---

## Usage

```
explorer.exe [/n] [,/root,object] [[/select],
subobject]
```

## Description

The Explorer is the default Windows shell. When run without any command-line parameters, it opens a two-paned window (commonly referred to simply as Explorer) in which you can navigate through all of the files, folders, and other resources on your computer.

Explorer accepts the following command-line options (note the mandatory commas):

/n    Forces Explorer to open a new window (even if the specified folder is already open somewhere).

/select,subobject
      Include subobject to specify the file or folder to be initially highlighted or expanded when the folder is opened. If subobject is a folder, it will be expanded in the tree. If you also include the /select parameter (not valid without subobject), the parent of the specified folder is highlighted on the tree, no branches are initially expanded, and subobject will be highlighted in the right pane.

,/root,object
      By default, Explorer opens with the Desktop as the root folder. Use ,/root,object to specify a different root. The object parameter can be a folder name or a class ID.

For example, if you want Explorer to open to the Computer folder so that no drive branches are initially expanded (which is handy if you have several drives), type the following:

```
explorer.exe /n, /select, c:\
```

To open an Explorer window rooted at the Documents folder, type:

```
explorer.exe /root,c:\Documents and Settings\username\
Documents
```

where username is the username of the owner of the Documents folder.

# Internet Explorer and Windows Mail

## Internet Explorer                    *\program files\internet explorer\iexplore.exe*

A web browser used to view web content.

### To open

Start → All Programs → Internet Explorer

Use the Internet Explorer icon on the Start menu or on the Quick Launch Toolbar.

Command Prompt → `iexplore`

### Usage

```
iexplore [-nohome] [url]
```

### Description

Internet Explorer is a full-featured web browser that you can use to navigate the Web, as well as view web content on your local network or hard drive. Web content is typically in the form of web pages (*.html*), but it can also be images (*.gif*, *.png*, and *.jpg*), FTP sites, or even streaming video or audio (via Windows Media Player).

You navigate in Internet Explorer by clicking hyperlinks in web pages or by typing addresses in Internet Explorer's Address Bar. You can "bookmark" frequently visited sites by creating Internet shortcuts (similar to Windows shortcuts), stored in your Favorites folder, your Desktop, or anywhere else on your hard disk.

Use the Back and Next buttons (as well as the Alt-left arrow and Alt-right arrow, respectively) to navigate through the history, which is empty in each new Internet Explorer window or tab that you open. Use the Stop button (or press the Esc key) to stop the loading of a page, and use the Refresh button (or press F5) to reload the page, displaying any changes that might have been made or displaying an updated version of a dynamically generated page.

The Home button loads the currently configured *home page(s)* into the browser window. The home page is merely a shortcut to a single web site, and you can change it by going to Tools → Internet Options.

If you start Internet Explorer from the command line or Start box, you can use either of the following options:

-nohome

Starts Internet Explorer without loading the home page (blank). You can also configure Internet Explorer to use a blank page (*about:blank*) as its home page, effectively causing Internet Explorer to always start without loading a home page.

*url*

The *Uniform Resource Locator*, which is the address of a page to load. If you omit *url*, Internet Explorer will display the home page.

## Content Tab and Content Advisor

Controls content you can view and use in Internet Explorer.

### To open

Internet Explorer → Tools → Internet Options → Content

### Description

This tab on the Internet Options dialog box controls a variety of miscellaneous content-related settings, including the Content Advisor, which can control the kind of web sites users of the PC are allowed to visit.

## Favorites Center

Revisit your favorite web sites and read RSS feeds.

### To open

Click the Favorites Center icon in Internet Explorer.

Press Alt-C when using Internet Explorer.

### Description

The Web is a massive, chaotic place, and it is difficult to remember all of your favorite web sites, much less be able to navigate quickly to them. That's where the Favorites Center comes in. It lets you organize all your favorite sites in a logical fashion, in folders, so that you can revisit them. It also lets you organize and read RSS feeds.

## Internet Options

Change the settings that affect Internet Explorer and your dial-up Internet connection.

## Page Menu

Performs a variety of functions on the current web page, including sending the page via email, changing the text size on the page, and copying text from the page.

### To open

Internet Explorer → Page

### Description

The Page menu is a catchall for letting you perform a wide variety of functions on the web page you're currently visiting. The topmost choices are self-explanatory and follow basic Vista conventions for copying, cutting, and pasting text, as well as opening a new window. (Note that when you open a new window, you're opening an entire new instance of Internet Explorer, not just a new tab. The new instance will be opened to the current web page.)

## RSS Feeds

Receive live feeds of web content, news, and weblogs (blogs).

## To open

Internet Explorer → Tools → Internet Options → Content → Feeds (to configure feeds)

Click the Feeds button in the Internet Explorer toolbar (to subscribe to feeds).

Click the Favorites Center in Internet Explorer, and choose the Feeds tab (to read feeds).

Internet Explorer 7, built into Vista, includes an RSS reader for subscribing to and reading RSS feeds. When you're on a page that has an RSS feed, the RSS icon on the Internet Explorer toolbar turns orange. Click the icon to read the feed using Internet Explorer's built-in RSS reader. In some cases, a web site has more than one feed on it. Click the inverted triangle next to the RSS icon and you'll see a list of all feeds on the site. Click the one you want to read.

## Search Bar

Searches the Internet using a variety of search providers.

## To open

Enter a search term in the Search Bar in the upper-righthand corner of Internet Explorer and press Enter, or click the magnifying glass icon.

## Tab Options

Control how Internet Explorer uses tabs.

## To open

Internet Explorer → Tools → Internet Options → General, then click Settings in the Tabs section

## Description

Probably the biggest visible change in the Vista version of Internet Explorer (and Internet Explorer 7 in XP) is the addition of tabs that allow you to browse multiple web sites simultaneously, each in its own tab. The Tab Options dialog box lets you control how Internet Explorer handles tabbed browsing.

## Internet Options Privacy Tab

Lets you take control over your privacy by controlling the way you manage cookies.

### To open

Internet Explorer → Tools Panel → Internet Options → Privacy

Command Prompt or Search Box → *inetcpl.cpl*, then click the Privacy tab

### Description

This tab lets you control how Internet Explorer handles cookies, small text files that web sites put on your hard disk to personalize the site for you or to track and record your activities on the site. As a means of site customization, they're a great way of helping you get the most out of the Web. They can also carry information about login names and passwords, which is a timesaver because you won't have to log in to each site every time you visit. If you delete all your cookies, you won't automatically get your Amazon wish list the next time you visit that site.

## Phishing Filter

Protect yourself against online scams and spoofs.

### To open

Internet Explorer → Tools → Phishing Filter

With Internet Explorer's phishing filter, when you try to visit what Microsoft deems a phishing site, Internet Explorer stops you in your tracks with a page warning you that you are about to head to a "reported phishing website." You then have the choice of closing the web site or ignoring the Microsoft recommendation and visiting it.

## Windows Mail                    *\Program Files\Windows Mail\WinMail.exe*

An Internet email client and newsgroup reader.

---

## To open

Start → All Programs → Windows Mail

Double-click the Windows Mail icon on the Desktop, if it's been enabled.

Command Prompt → `winmail`

## Description

Windows Mail uses a familiar Explorer-like tree interface to manage the folders into which email and newsgroup messages are organized. Highlight any folder name to display its messages; the currently highlighted message is then shown in the preview pane. Double-click the message to open it in a new window for easier reading and other options.

Newly received messages are stored in the Inbox folder. Files queued to be sent are stored in the Outbox folder, and are then moved to the Sent Items folder when they have been sent. The Deleted Items folder is like the Recycle Bin because it stores deleted messages until it is emptied manually. The Drafts folder stores messages as they're being composed. To add a new folder, select Local Folders in the tree and go to File → New → Folder. You can move messages from folder to folder by dragging and dropping them.

# Networking, Wireless, and Mobility

## Connect to a Network

Connect to a network or the Internet.

## To open

Click the network icon in the System Tray → Connect or disconnect

Control Panel → [Network and Internet] → Connect to a network

Control Panel → [Network and Internet] → Network and Sharing Center → Connect to a network

### Description

Once you've set up a network connection, use the "Connect to a network" screen to connect to any network—wired, wireless, VPN, or dial-up.

Connecting is straightforward: double-click the network to which you want to connect, or highlight it and click Connect. When you're connected to a network, disconnect from it by clicking Disconnect.

This screen is primarily designed for wireless, dial-up, and VPN connections. If your only connection to a network is via an Ethernet cable, you won't even get to the screen when you choose to connect. Instead, you'll be told that you're already connected to the network. Want to disconnect? There's a simple, physical solution for you—unplug your Ethernet cable.

## Manage Network Connections          *\windows\system\ncpa.cpl*

Configure and manage your network connections.

### To open

Control Panel → [Network and Internet] → Network and Sharing Center → Manage network connections

Command prompt → `ncpa.cpl`

### Description

Manage Network Connections is actually a specialized folder that lists and provides details about all of your network connections, and lets you configure and manage them. Click any network connection and a toolbar appears that lets you take a variety of actions on the connection, including connecting it, disabling the network device, renaming the connection, viewing the status of the connection, changing the connection's settings, and diagnosing problems with the connection.

## Manage Wireless Networks

Configure and manage wireless networks.

**To open**

Control Panel → [Network and Internet] → Network and Sharing Center → Manage wireless networks

**Description**

Many people regularly connect to more than one wireless network—one at home, one at work, and possibly more than one public hotspot. When you create a wireless connection, you have the option of saving that network as a connection; any networks that you've saved will show up on the Manage Wireless Networks screen.

## Network Connection Properties (Includes Wired and Wireless Connections)

Configure network services associated with a network connection.

**To open**

Control Panel → [Network and Internet] → Network and Sharing Center → View Status → Properties

**Description**

The Network Connection Properties screen lists all the installed protocols and services associated with a network connection (both wired and wireless). It provides you with basic information about your wireless connection to help with troubleshooting, and it helps you configure your network and its connection. You can selectively choose which protocols and services are supported by any specific connection by using the checkboxes in the list.

## Network Map

Display a "live" map of your network.

**To open**

Control Panel → [Network and Internet] → Network and Sharing Center → View full map

### Description

The Network Map feature shows a detailed schematic of your network and all the devices connected to it. The map is "live"—that is, the icons are not merely representations, but also perform actions and provide information. Hover your mouse over a device and you'll get information about that device; for example, hover your mouse over a gateway to see its IP address and MAC address (a MAC address is a unique identifier for network hardware, a kind of serial number). Click a PC, and you'll connect to it and see all the shared network files and folders in Windows Explorer. Click the Internet icon, and you'll launch your default browser to your home page.

## Network and Sharing Center

Configure, customize, and access network and collaboration tools.

### To open

Control Panel → [Network and Internet] → Network and Sharing Center

### Description

The Network and Sharing Center lets you configure, access, and troubleshoot a wide variety of network features. You'll most likely find that it's the primary place you'll turn for handling network issues, configuring networks, troubleshooting networks, and performing other network-related tasks.

Front and center is a brief diagram of your network, showing your computer name and how it connects to your local network, and then to the Internet. Think of it as a kind of "you-are-here" diagram, because you'll see the words "This computer" underneath your computer. The diagram is so basic that at first it appears it may be useless, but in fact, you'll find it surprisingly useful. The diagram is "live" so that if there's a problem with your network or Internet connection, you'll be notified here. In addition, you can click on the icons representing the different portions of your network and connect to them. For example, click your computer's icon, and you'll open Windows Explorer to your Computer folder. Click the Network icon to open Windows Explorer to the Network folder, which lists all of the computers on your network. Click Internet to open Internet Explorer to your home page.

## Set Up a Connection or Network

Set up a new network or Internet connection.

### To open

Control Panel → [Network and Internet] → Network and Sharing Center → Set up a connection or network

### Description

One of the reasons that networking in Windows Vista is so much easier than working in previous Windows versions is this wizard. Answer a series of questions, and you can set up a new network or connection in minutes.

## Network Connection Status

Get details about a network connection.

### To open

Control Panel → [Network and Internet] → Network and Sharing Center → View Status

Control Panel → [Network and Internet] → Network and Sharing Center → Manage network connections → Right-click a connection and select Status

### Description

You can use this screen for wired and wireless networks, although it will be used more frequently for wireless networks because wireless connections require more care and handling than wired connections. They are more apt to be slow because of interference problems, and to disconnect due to interference and other problems. And you're likely to have multiple wireless connections set up on your PC—one for work, one for home, and several for your favorite hotspots.

The Network Connection Status screen provides you with basic information about your connection to help with troubleshooting, and to help you configure your network and its connection.

## Remote Desktop Connection     *\windows\system32\mstsc.exe*

Access another computer remotely and use it as though you are sitting in front of it.

### To open

Start → All Programs → Accessories → Remote Desktop Connection

Command Prompt → `mstsc`

### Description

Remote Desktop Connection allows you to connect to another computer (or allows someone else to connect to your computer) and use it as though you were sitting in front of it. Much more than simply a remote command prompt (like SSH or Telnet), Remote Desktop Connection allows you to see a full Desktop, complete with icons and the Start menu, and even run programs on the remote computer.

## Offline Files

Work with files stored on a network when you're not connected to it.

### To open

Control Panel → [Network and Internet] → Offline Files

### Description

The Offline Files dialog lets you turn on (and off) and configure Windows Vista's Offline Files feature, which allows you to work with files stored on a network (either server-based or peer-to-peer), when you're not actually connected to the network. Windows XP also had the capability to work with offline files, but it was so confusing to use and configure that people rarely used it. In Windows Vista, the Offline Files dialog and the Sync Center make the use of offline files far easier. If you use a laptop to connect to your network and would like the ability to work with those files when you're not connected, it's an extremely useful feature.

## Power Options

*\windows\system\powercfg.cpl*

Select a power plan for your laptop.

### To open

Control Panel → Change battery settings

Control Panel → [Mobile PC] → Power Options

Right-click the battery icon → Power Options

Command Prompt → **powercfg.cpl**

### Description

When you use a laptop, you're always balancing the need to save power against laptop performance. You want to use the computer as long as possible on a battery charge (for example, if you're on a cross-country airplane trip), but you also want to be as productive as possible when using it.

The Power Options Control Panel lets you choose a power plan for your laptop, customize power plans, and change a variety of other power options.

## Sync Center

*\windows\system32\mobsync.exe*

Synchronize files and folders with devices and network folders.

### To open

Control Panel → [Mobile PC] → Sync Center

Control Panel → [Network and Internet] → Sync Center

Command Prompt → **mobsync**

## Description

If you have multimedia devices such as MP3 players and iPods, have portable storage devices such as USB flash drives, or work on files on multiple PCs, you know how hard it is to keep all your files in sync on those devices and computers. The Sync Center is Windows Vista's answer. It's the central location for syncing all your devices and network folders.

When devices and network folders are synced, Windows Vista copies and updates files and folders in both locations. So, for example, if you've made changes to files on both your PC and the device, Windows Vista will perform actions on both of them so that they have identical files and folders.

You can also use the Sync Center for synchronizing files across a network, via offline files. With offline files, you can get access to files on a shared network folder, even if your laptop is not currently connected to the network. Offline files allow you to open files, work on them when you're disconnected, and then update them at a later time when the connection has been reestablished.

# Windows Mobility Center

Control commonly used mobility settings.

## To open

Control Panel → Mobile PC → Windows Mobility Center

## Description

The Windows Mobility Center Panel offers quick access to turn on and off and customize a variety of commonly used mobility settings.

# Security

## Parental Controls

Controls the way children can use the computer and the Internet.

### To open

Control Panel → [User Accounts and Family Safety] → Parental Controls

Control Panel → [User Accounts and Family Safety] → Set up parental controls for any user

Control Panel → Set up parental controls for any user

Control Panel → [Security] → Parental Controls

Control Panel → [Security] → Set up parental controls for any user

### Description

Many parents are justifiably worried about how their children use computers and the Internet. The Internet can be a dangerous place for children—particularly young children, preteens, and even teens. They may inadvertently come across pornography, violent images, or other unsuitable content, and they could even be targeted by predators.

In addition, parents may want to block access to certain programs on a shared PC—giving children access to your personal finance software, for example, could prove to be disastrous.

## Security Center                                        *wscui.cpl*

Provides easy access to the Windows Firewall, antivirus and anti-malware settings, Windows Update, and other security settings.

## To open

Control Panel → Security → Security Center

Command Prompt → `wscui.cpl`

## Description

The Security Center doesn't actually provide any additional security, but it does act as a control center for your existing software—keeping tabs on what's on or off and what needs updating or replacing, and providing impossible-to-miss warnings that erupt from the Windows notification area. You'll get a warning from the System Tray if the Security Center detects that something is amiss with your security; otherwise, the Security Center won't appear there.

---

### TIP

Don't confuse the Security Center with the Security Control Panel category. The Security Control Panel category includes links to a wider variety of security settings and controls than does the Security Center. The Security Center's main purpose is to issue alerts and warnings about your security settings, not to provide a front door to every security feature in Windows Vista—for example, it doesn't link to BitLocker Encryption and Parental Controls like the Security Control Panel category does.

---

The Security Center keeps an eye on firewalls (Windows Vista's own or any Windows Vista-compliant third-party program), your antivirus software, your antispyware software, your Internet security settings, UAC, and the Automatic Updates feature in Windows. The Center will pop up an alert if it thinks there's a problem in any of these areas. You can turn off monitoring by clicking the "Change the way Security Center alerts me" link in the main Security Center window. Note that the Security Center monitors your software only for activation and updates—it doesn't actually provide any security itself.

## User Account Control

Protects users against threats by controlling access to important settings.

### To open

User Account Control is turned on by default.

### Description

User Account Control (UAC), new to Vista, is designed to protect users against a variety of threats, but it is by far the most controversial change to the operating system. The feature caused enough outcry during the beta (testing) phase of Windows Vista that Microsoft changed how it works several times.

Like it or not, though, UAC is here to stay, and it offers substantially increased security over previous versions of Windows. It is designed to prevent unauthorized changes to your computer so that the system and its files cannot be damaged or tampered with. This protection is designed not only against external threats and malware, but also against users of the computer who accidentally make dangerous changes.

## Windows Update

Automatically downloads and installs updates to Windows Vista over the Internet.

### To open

Control Panel → [Security] → Windows Update

Control Panel → Check for Updates

Start → All Programs → Windows Update

### Description

Windows Update downloads and installs updates to Windows Vista quickly and easily. These updates are important because they often contain security patches that plug holes found in the operating system.

By default, Windows Update is turned on in Windows Vista. Windows Vista checks for new updates daily. It categorizes three types of updates: important updates, recommended updates, and optional updates. Important updates include security and critical performance updates. Recommended updates are those that help fix or prevent problems. Optional updates are less important updates, such as new or updated drivers. Optional updates are not automatically installed, but Windows Update will list any available and let you download and install them if you want.

## Windows Defender     *\Program Files\Windows Defender\MSASCui.exe*

Protect your PC against spyware, home-page hijackers, and other threats.

### To open

Start → Control Panel → Security → Windows Defender

Double-click the Windows Defender icon in the System Tray.

Command Prompt → **\Program Files\Windows Defender\ MSASCui.exe**

Windows Defender offers you automatic protection against spyware. It runs in the background as you use your computer, and it is designed to stop spyware before it infects your computer. When a piece of spyware attempts to install itself, hijack your home page, or do other damage, Windows Defender deletes the software and puts it into a quarantine area, where you can examine it later on. Should you decide that Windows Defender deleted the software in error, you can restore it.

## BitLocker Drive Encryption

Encrypts entire drives so that data can't be read, even if your computer is stolen (available only with the Enterprise and Ultimate editions of Windows Vista).

### To open

Control Panel → [Security] → BitLocker Drive Encryption

## Description

BitLocker Drive Encryption, new to Windows Vista, is the best way to keep all of your files safe from others. It works even if you have a laptop and it's stolen. It's designed so that your laptop or PC won't even start up without your encryption key, so a thief will not even be able to boot your PC, much less read any of its files. BitLocker Drive Encryption encrypts all files on a drive, including those needed for startup and logon. By doing this, it ensures that a thief cannot start your system, log on to it, and then steal your encrypting password as a way to decrypt and read your files.

BitLocker encrypts all new files you add to your protected drive. The files are encrypted only when they are stored on the drive you've encrypted. If you copy them to another drive or computer, they are automatically decrypted. Shared files are encrypted when they are stored on the encrypted drive, and any user who has access to BitLocker-protected shared files will be able to use them as she would normally.

# Hardware

## Add Hardware Wizard                    *\windows\system\hdwwiz.cpl*

Detect non-Plug and Play devices and install the appropriate drivers.

### To open

Control Panel → Add Hardware (in Classic view)

Command Prompt → **hdwwiz.cpl**

### Description

When you turn on your computer, Windows automatically scans for newly added Plug and Play (PnP) devices and installs drivers for any that it finds. If you're trying to install a device that isn't detected automatically, you'll need to run the Add Hardware Wizard.

When you start the Add Hardware Wizard and click Next, it goes through the following steps:

1. You're asked whether to have the wizard search for and install the hardware automatically, or whether you want to choose the hardware from a list. It's best to have the wizard search automatically.

2. The wizard scans your system for any newly attached PnP devices. If one or more devices are found, the appropriate drivers are located and installed.

3. If no new devices are found in step 2 (or if you decide in step 1 to choose hardware from a list), you'll be asked to click Next to choose your hardware from a list.

4. The wizard displays a list of hardware categories from which you can choose ("Display adapters," "Imaging devices," "All devices," and so on). Select a category. A list of manufacturers appears. Select the manufacturer.

5. If you have the drivers for the device on either a floppy, a CD, or your hard disk, click Have Disk at this point. Otherwise, choose the specific model number from the list on the right. If your device doesn't show up here, drivers for it aren't included with Windows Vista.

6. The last steps involve copying and installing the drivers, and then prompting you to restart (if applicable).

## AutoPlay

Set options for how Windows handles the insertion of various types of media and content.

### To open

Control Panel → [Hardware and Sound] → AutoPlay

### Description

Whenever you insert a CD or DVD in your PC, Windows either takes an action or asks you what action it should take. AutoPlay lets you set how Windows should handle many different types of media—and can even take different actions based on the media's content.

Configuration is straightforward. For each type of media or content, select the action you want Windows to take when the media or content is inserted and then click Save.

## Device Manager                      \windows\system32\devmgmt.msc

Configure all hardware installed in or attached to a computer.

### To open

Control Panel → [System and Maintenance] → Device Manager

Control Panel → [System and Maintenance] → System → Device Manager

Control Panel → [Hardware and Sound] → Device Manager

Command Prompt → **devmgmt.msc**

### Description

Device Manager is the central interface for gathering information about and making changes to all the hardware installed in a system. Device Manager has an Explorer-style tree listing all of the various hardware categories; expand any category branch to display all installed devices that fit in that category. For example, expand the Network adapters branch to list all installed network cards in the system.

## Disk and Volume Properties

View and change the properties of disks and volumes, including removable disks.

### To open

Right-click a drive → Properties

Click a drive → Organize → Properties

### Description

The exact number of tabs on the Disk Properties page varies according to the type of drive or volume and its characteristics. For example, a hard drive may have seven tabs: General, Tools,

Hardware, Sharing, Security, Previous Versions, and Customize. A USB flash drive, on the other hand, may have six: General, Tools, Hardware, Sharing, ReadyBoost, and Customize. And a DVD-RW drive may have five: General, Hardware, Sharing, Customize, and Recording.

---

**TIP**

There is a difference between a physical disk and a volume, although Windows Vista calls them both disks. The physical disk is the hardware itself, and a volume is a separate section of the hard disk. So a single disk may have multiple volumes, or it may have only a single volume.

---

## Display Settings                   \windows\system32\desk.cpl

Change the settings of your display adapter and monitor.

### To open

Control Panel → [Appearance and Personalization] → Adjust screen resolution

Control Panel → [Appearance and Personalization] → Personalization → Display Settings

Right-click on an empty portion of your Desktop → Personalize → Display Settings

Command Prompt → **desk.cpl**

### Description

This dialog lets you choose the resolution and color depth of your screen, change your display hardware settings, and customize how you use two monitors on the same system. Two limitations of your video card may affect the settings here. First, the amount of memory on your video card dictates the maximum color depth and resolution you can use. Second, as you adjust your color depth, Windows may automatically adjust other settings depending on your card's capabilities. If you increase your color depth, your resolution might automatically decrease; likewise, if you raise the resolution, your color depth might go down.

---

If you have more than one monitor, using either two separate video cards or a single video card that supports two monitors, all configured screens will be shown in the preview area. Click any screen icon to activate it; the settings below apply only to the selected monitor. You can even drag and drop monitor icons to rearrange them so that, for example, a different monitor assumes the role of the upper left. If you're not sure which monitor is #1 and which is #2, click Identify Monitors.

## Keyboard Properties

Change the keyboard repeat rate and text cursor blink rate.

### To open

Control Panel → [Hardware and Sound] → Keyboard

Command Prompt → `control main.cpl Keyboard`

Command Prompt → `control keyboard`

### Description

The Keyboard Properties dialog controls the way characters are repeated when keys are held down, as well as how quickly the text cursor (insertion point) blinks. Tip: move the "Repeat rate" slider all the way to the right (toward Fast), and your computer may actually seem faster.

## Mouse Properties                    \windows\system32\main.cpl

Change settings that affect the behavior of your pointing device and the appearance of the mouse cursor.

### To open

Control Panel → [Hardware and Sound] → Mouse

Command Prompt → `control main.cpl`

Command Prompt → `control mouse`

### Description

The Mouse Properties dialog controls the buttons and motion of your pointing device and the appearance of the various mouse cursors, such as the arrow and hourglass.

---

## Printers

Manage printers.

### To open

Control Panel → [Hardware and Sound] → Printers

### Description

Printers is actually a specialized Windows Explorer folder that offers a variety of ways to manage your printers and printing. The folder lists all of your printers and includes a toolbar for managing them, including adding a printer, opening the print queue, choosing printing preferences, pausing a printer, renaming and deleting a printer, sharing a printer, and so on.

Many of the same options are also available when you right-click a printer. To set a printer as the default, right-click it and choose Set as Default Printer.

---

## Scanners and Cameras

Displays and configures scanners and digital cameras.

### To open

Control Panel → [Hardware and Sound] → Scanners and Cameras

### Description

The Scanners and Cameras window lists any digital cameras or scanners attached to the system.

If you have a scanner or digital camera attached to your system and it's not showing up, click Refresh. If it still doesn't show up, click Add Device, and the Scanner and Camera Installation Wizard appears. It is, in fact, the same wizard as the Add Hardware Wizard, so just follow those instructions.

---

## Sound Recorder                    *\windows\system32\SoundRecorder.exe*

Record and play sound files.

### To open

Start → All Programs → Accessories → Sound Recorder

Command Prompt → **Soundrecorder**

### Description

You use the Sound Recorder to record simple sound clips, either in Windows Media Audio (*.wma*) or Waveform audio (*.wav*) format, depending on your version of Windows Vista. Windows Vista Basic and Windows Vista record sound files as *.wav* files, and all other versions record sound files as *.wma* files.

Unlike the Sound Recorder in Windows XP, the Windows Vista version only records sounds and cannot play them back or edit them. (For playing them back, use Windows Media Player.) There are virtually no controls. Click Start Recording to begin recording sound; click Stop Recording to stop and save the sound, or click Resume Recording after you've stopped to continue recording where you left off.

---

## Volume Mixer

Control the volume of sound devices.

### To open

Control Panel → [Hardware and Sound] → Adjust System Volume

Notification Area → Right-click the speaker icon and choose Open Volume Mixer

Notification Area → Left-click the speaker icon and choose Mixer

### Description

The Volume Mixer lets you change the volume of your current speakers or other audio device, as well as the volume of sounds for Windows system events and for individual applications that use sounds for notifications and warnings. If you have multiple applications running, you can change their volumes independently of one another, through separate sliders.

## Windows Update Driver Settings

Control how Windows finds new drivers.

### To open

Right-click Computer on Start menu → Properties → Advanced System Settings → Hardware → Windows Update Driver Settings

Control Panel → [System and Maintenance] → System, then click Change Settings → Hardware → Windows Update Driver Settings

Command Prompt → `sysdm.cpl` → Hardware → Windows Update Driver Settings

### Description

When you connect a new device to your PC, Windows finds and installs the driver by default. The Windows Update Driver Settings dialog lets you change that behavior. You can have Windows ask each time before checking for drivers, or not check at all.

## XPS Document Viewer

View documents in the new *.xps* format.

### To open

Double-click any file in the *.xps* format.

### Description

The new XML Paper Specification (XPS), introduced with Windows Vista, is Microsoft's answer to Adobe's popular Portable Document Format (*.pdf*). It displays a document with all of its layout, fonts, and graphics intact. Any Windows application can create a *.xps* file by printing as it would normally, except choosing the Microsoft XPS Document Writer as the printer and then saving the results on disk to an *.xps* file. XPS documents can be read but not edited.

Windows Vista's built-in XPS Document Viewer runs as a specialized instance of Internet Explorer.

# Managing Programs, Users, and Your Computer

## Group Policy Object Editor          *\windows\system32\gpedit.msc*

Refresh group policies and settings.

### To open

Command Prompt → **gpedit.msc** (not available in Home versions)

### Description

The Group Policy Object Editor offers tools that go far beyond anything offered in the Control Panel—or anywhere else in Windows, for that matter—affecting settings that most users have never even heard of. It gives a system administrator the ability to create a variety of policies for individual machines and users, quickly rolling them out across a network and relying on Windows Vista for enforcement. However, although it was primarily designed for system managers on networks, it can be very useful for single machines as well, not only for creating policies for every user of the single computer, but also for offering access to settings and controls not otherwise accessible.

Unlike the Registry, which presents its arcane settings in a mountain of folders and subfolders, the Group Policy Object Editor's options are shown in a handful of folders in (sometimes) plain English, such as "Hide/Add New Programs Page" and "Turn off Windows Sidebar." (And there are obscure ones as well, such as "User Group Policy loopback processing mode.") Although the presentation is different, most settings here are implemented as changes to values and keys in your Registry.

## Logoff          *\windows\system32\logoff.exe*

Log off the current user (or another user).

### To open

Command Prompt → **logoff**

## Usage

```
logoff [session | id] [/server:name] [/v]
```

## Description

Among other things, Logoff is the quickest way to log off the current user, rather than clicking the Start Menu, then clicking the right arrow on its right edge, then selecting Log Off. In fact, you can create a shortcut to Logoff on your Desktop and simply double-click it to end the current session.

---

## Microsoft Management Console    \windows\system32\mmc.exe

A single interface for dozens of administrative tools in Windows Vista.

### To open

Start → All Programs → Administrative Tools → Computer Management

Command Prompt → **mmc**

### Usage

```
mmc filename [/a] [/64] [/32]
```

### Description

The Microsoft Management Console (MMC) is a host for most of the administrative tools that come with Windows Vista. Each tool that works with the MMC is called a snap-in; several snap-ins can be shown in the MMC at any given time, and they appear as entries in the Explorer-style tree in the left pane.

You can save a collection of one or more snap-ins into a Console (.msc) file, which is a small file that simply lists snap-ins to display in the Console window. Double-click any .msc file to open it in the MMC. Windows Vista ships with more than two dozen predefined Console files, and you can modify them (or even create your own) by adding or removing snap-ins or creating custom Taskpad Views—pages with lists of shortcuts to programs or other snap-ins.

---

## User Accounts

Add, remove, and customize user accounts and change the privileges of existing users.

### To open

Control Panel → [User Accounts and Family Safety] → User Accounts

Command Prompt → **control userpasswords**

### Description

Windows Vista fully supports multiple users, each with his own Start menu, Desktop, color and display theme preferences, application settings, folder for documents, music, downloads, pictures, saved games, and a variety of other odds and ends. Each user has a password and a home directory (located in *\Users\username*), under which his personal files and folders are stored by default. The user, of course, can create folders outside of that home directory if he wants.

Windows Vista lets you create separate accounts not only as a way to let multiple people share the same PC, but also for security reasons. It has several different kinds of user accounts, each with its own level of privileges for performing tasks such as installing and uninstalling software, changing system settings, and so on, and Windows Vista uses these differences in privileges for security purposes with its User Account Control (UAC) feature, described earlier in the chapter.

There are two basic kinds of user accounts in Windows Vista:

*Administrator*
   An administrator has control over the entire system and can run programs, install or remove hardware and software, change system settings, and create, remove, and modify other user accounts. There doesn't have to be just one administrator; there can be multiple administrators on a single PC.

*Standard user*
   A standard user is more limited in what he can do on the computer than an administrator and may not be able to

change various system settings, install and uninstall hardware and software, access certain files and folders, and so on. There can be multiple standard users on a single PC.

## Calculator                                       \windows\system32\calc.exe

Numerical scientific and nonscientific calculator.

### To open

Start → All Programs → Accessories → Calculator

Command Prompt → `calc`

### Description

By default, the Calculator starts in Standard mode, containing only the numeric keypad and some basic functions (add, subtract, invert, square root, etc.). Select Scientific from the View menu to use the calculator in Scientific mode, useful for more advanced functions, such as logarithmic, logical, trigonometric, and base functions. Each time you subsequently open the Calculator, it will appear in the previously used mode.

## Character Map                              \windows\system32\charmap.exe

Display all the characters and symbols in a particular font. This provides access to symbols not easily accessible with the keyboard.

### To open

Start → All Programs → Accessories → System Tools → Character Map

Command Prompt → `charmap`

### Description

Character Map displays a visual map of all the characters in any font, making it easy to paste them into other documents.

## Default Programs Control Panel

Change a variety of program-related settings, including specifying the default programs to use for various file types and protocols, changing AutoPlay settings, and controlling access to certain programs.

### To open

Start → Default programs

### Description

By default, certain programs are associated with certain file types and protocols and will automatically launch when those files and protocols are opened. For example, by default Internet Explorer opens all *.html* files and Windows Contacts opens all *.vcf* files—vCard files that contain contact information. So whenever you double-click to open either of those file types—in Windows Explorer, in Windows Mail, or anywhere else—the default program will launch and open the file.

The Default Programs Control Panel lets you make changes to those defaults, and lets you change a variety of other settings as well, such as whether CDs, DVDs, and other media should auto-play when inserted.

## Microsoft Magnifier                    *\windows\system32\magnify.exe*

Show an enlarged version of the area of the screen near the mouse cursor.

### To open

Start → All Programs → Accessories → Ease of Access → Magnifier

Command Prompt → **magnify**

### Description

The Microsoft Magnifier is used to assist those with visual impairments by magnifying a portion of the screen. When you start

Magnifier, the top 15 percent of the screen turns into an automatic magnifying glass, which follows the mouse cursor around the screen. If you have trouble seeing something on the screen, just float the cursor over it to magnify it.

## Notepad

\windows\notepad.exe

A rudimentary plain-text editor.

### To open

Start → All Programs → Accessories → Notepad

Command Prompt → **notepad**

### Usage

```
notepad [/p] [filename]
```

### Description

Notepad is one of the simplest yet most useful tools included with Windows Vista. Those familiar with word processors may find Notepad to be laughably limited at first glance, as it has no support for even the simplest formatting. However, the fact that it supports only text in the documents that it creates is an absolute necessity for many of the tasks for which it is used on a daily basis.

## Program Compatibility Wizard

Configure older programs to help them run under Windows Vista.

### To open

Control Panel → Programs → Use an older program with this version of Windows

### Description

Old programs, especially old DOS-based programs and games, may have problems running under Windows Vista. The Program Compatibility Wizard helps you troubleshoot problems with those programs, and help them run under Windows Vista.

## Uninstall or Change a Program   \windows\system32\appwiz.cpl

Uninstall programs, or add or remove extra program features.

### To open

Control Panel → Programs → Programs and Features

Command Prompt → **appwiz.cpl**

### Description

This Control Panel applet lets you uninstall any program on your PC, as well as change the program by adding new features, or repair the program if for some reason it has been damaged.

To uninstall a program, double-click it and follow the prompts that appear. (You can also right-click it and choose Uninstall.) To add new features or remove features from the program, right-click it and select Change. In many instances, you'll need the CD or DVD from which you installed the program in order to add—and sometimes remove—features. You'll be prompted for the CD or DVD. Right-click and choose Repair to fix a damaged program—and again, you'll usually need the CD or DVD installation disk to do that.

## WordPad   \Program Files\Windows NT\Accessories\wordpad.exe

A simple word processor.

### To open

Start → All Programs → Accessories → WordPad

Command Prompt → C:\Program Files\Windows NT\Accessories\ wordpad.exe

### Description

Although WordPad lacks many of the features that come with full-blown word processors such as WordPerfect and Microsoft Word, it has enough features to let you create and edit rich-text documents. WordPad is the default editor for .rtf and .wri files (unless Microsoft Word is installed). You also can use WordPad to edit plain-text files (.txt), although Notepad (discussed earlier in this chapter) is the default and is more appropriate for this task.

# Performance and Troubleshooting

## Backup and Restore Center

Back up (copy) files from your hard drive to a CD drive, DVD drive, removable storage device, or another PC or drive on a network for the purpose of safeguarding or archiving your data, or for saving your computer configuration so that you can restore it in the event of a crash.

### To open

Control Panel → Back up your computer

Control Panel → System and Maintenance → Backup and Restore Center

### Description

The Backup and Restore Center, new in Windows Vista, offers tools for backing up data as well as creating a restore "image" of your computer, which can be used to re-create the state of your PC—including the operating system, applications, and settings—in the event of a hardware failure. It fixes a variety of shortcomings in the backup program built into Windows XP, such as not being able to back up across a network. On the other hand, it's less flexible than the XP backup program because it doesn't allow you to customize it to a great extent. You can't, for example, choose specific folders, or files from specific folders, to be backed up. Instead, you have to back up all files of a particular file type, such as documents.

## Computer

Shows an overview of all your system's drives.

### To open

Start → Computer

Start → All Programs → Accessories → System Tools → Computer

### Description

Gives a quick overview of all of your computer's drives and folders in Windows Explorer.

---

## Computer Management                    *\windows\system32\compmgmt.msc*

Perform computer management tasks and run tools such as the Task Scheduler.

### To open

Run as a plug-in for the Microsoft Management Console.

Command Prompt → `compmgmt`

### Description

This plug-in to the Microsoft Management Console lets you perform a variety of computer management tasks, including monitoring performance and reliability. It also provides a way to run tools such as the Task Scheduler.

---

## Disk Cleanup                    *\windows\system32\cleanmgr.exe*

Reclaim disk space by removing unwanted files from your hard drive.

### To open

Start → All Programs → Accessories → System Tools → Disk Cleanup

Control Panel → [System and Maintenance] → Free up disk space

Command Prompt → `cleanmgr`

### Description

Disk Cleanup summarizes the disk space used by several predefined types of files, such as Temporary Internet Files and items in the Recycle Bin. If you have more than one hard drive, Disk Cleanup prompts you to choose one. It also asks whether you want to clean up only your files, or files from all users on the computer (you'll need Administrator rights to do the latter).

---

## Disk Defragmenter

*\windows\system32\dfrgui.exe*

Reorganize the files on a disk to optimize disk performance and reliability.

### To open

Control Panel → [System and Maintenance ] → Defragment your hard drive

Command Prompt → **dfrgui**

### Description

As you create files on your hard disk, they become defragmented so that a single file is stored in several different noncontiguous locations. As more files become fragmented, the reliability and performance of the hard drive diminish. Disk Defragmenter reorganizes the files and folders on a drive so that the files are stored contiguously, and the free space is contiguous as well.

## DiskPart

*\windows\system32\diskpart.exe*

Prepare and partition a hard disk.

### To open

Command Prompt → **diskpart**

### Description

DiskPart is a full-featured program used to prepare hard disks and, optionally, divide them into two or more partitions. It's a command-line program and has no interface to speak of. When you start DiskPart, you'll see a simple prompt: DISKPART>. Type **help** and press Enter to view a list of all the available commands.

## Event Viewer

*\windows\system32\eventvwr.msc*

Read system logs and view other system events.

### To open

Run as a plug-in for the Microsoft Management Console.

Command Prompt → `eventvwr`

### Description

A plug-in to the Microsoft Management Console, the Event Viewer provides an easy way to read system logs and view other system events.

## Performance Information and Tools

Rate your computer's capability to run Windows Vista.

### To open

Control Panel → System and Maintenance → Performance Information and Tools

### Description

This screen rates your PC according to how well it runs Windows, using what it calls a Windows Experience Index. It rates the processor, RAM, graphics subsystem, gaming graphics subsystem, and primary hard disk on a scale of one to five. The higher the number, the better the performance. The lowest rating of any of those is called the system's Base Score.

## Performance Options

Controls the balance between using advanced Windows Vista visual features and performance.

### To open

Control Panel → [System and Maintenance] → System → Advanced System Settings → Advanced, click Settings under Performance

### Description

Windows Vista contains a great deal of "eye candy" that makes using the operating system a far more visually pleasing experience. But on some systems, these visual effects can slow a system down. Use Performance Options to balance visual effects against performance.

## Problem Reports and Solutions

Automatically solve problems with your computer and Windows Vista.

### To open

Control Panel → [System and Maintenance] → Problem Reports and Solutions

### Description

One of the best new troubleshooting features in Windows Vista is its capability to automatically detect problems with your computer and offer automated fixes for them. The Control Panel's Problem Reports and Solutions applet is the place to go to find and launch these solutions.

The applet displays any solutions to install, as well as information about problems that do not yet have solutions, are not serious enough to require solutions, or will have solutions. Click any to launch a wizard that walks you through the steps to fix the problem.

## ReadyBoost

Speeds up computer performance by storing commonly used files in a flash device.

### Description

ReadyBoost, new to Windows Vista, uses a flash memory device (USB stick, SD card, etc.) to prefetch and store commonly used files, and essentially treats the device as a way to augment RAM. It's an inexpensive and easy way to speed up Windows Vista performance.

ReadyBoost speeds up Windows Vista performance in several ways. It increases the size of the prefetch cache, and it frees up RAM that would otherwise be used by prefetch. Depending on your system configuration, you may see a dramatic speed improvement.

To use ReadyBoost, connect a flash drive to your PC. Windows Vista will recognize the device, and then it will ask whether to use it to speed up your PC with ReadyBoost or use it as a normal drive. Select "Speed up my system" and ReadyBoost goes into action, without further intervention required on your part.

## Reliability and Performance Monitor   *\windows\system32\perfmon.msc*
*or \windows\system32\perfmon.exe*

Track and review system performance.

### To open

Run as a plug-in for the Microsoft Management Console.

Command Prompt → **perfmon**

### Description

This plug-in to the Microsoft Management Console tracks system performance and shows a history of application, Windows, hardware, and miscellaneous failures, as well as software installations and uninstallations. Go to any day for details for the failures, installations, and uninstallations for that day. The graph displays the overall reliability over time, so you can see whether your computer is becoming less reliable as it ages.

## System Information   *\windows\system32\msinfo32.exe*

Collect and display information about your computer.

### To open

Start → All Programs → Accessories → System Tools → System Information

Command Prompt → **msinfo32**

## Description

Microsoft System Information is a reporting tool used to view information about hardware, system resources used by that hardware, software drivers, and Internet Explorer settings. Information is arranged in a familiar Explorer-like tree. Expand or collapse branches with the little plus (+) and minus (–) signs, and click any category to view the corresponding information in the righthand pane.

## Services                                 *\windows\system32\services.msc*

Manage system services.

### To open

Run as a plug-in for the Microsoft Management Console.

Command Prompt → **services**

### Description

This plug-in to the Microsoft Management Console displays system services and lets you start and stop services, control whether they run at startup, and customize how they run.

## System Control Panel

Get basic information about your computer.

### To open

Control Panel → [System and Maintenance] → System

### Description

The System Control Panel shows you at a glance basic information about your computer, including the type of processor and speed, installed RAM, Windows Vista edition, computer name, product ID, and more.

The panel also includes a variety of links to settings, such as System Properties.

## System Properties                    \windows\system32\sysdm.cpl

View and modify many general Windows settings.

### To open

Control Panel → [System and Maintenance] → System, then click Change settings

Command Prompt → **control sysdm.cpl**

### Description

The System Properties window contains settings that affect hardware, system performance, networking, and other Windows features.

## System Protection and System Restore

\windows\system32\restore\rstrui.exe

(System Restore only)

Roll back your computer's configuration to an earlier state, with the intention of undoing potentially harmful changes.

### To open

Start → All Programs → Accessories → System Tools → System Restore

Control Panel → [System and Maintenance] → System → System Protection

Command Prompt → **rstrui**

### Description

System Protection (also confusingly called System Restore) is a feature that runs invisibly in the background, continuously backing up important system files and Registry settings. The idea is that at some point, you may want to roll back your computer's configuration to a time before things started going wrong. By default, System Restore is turned on, using at least 300 MB of your computer's hard-disk space.

System Restore is particularly useful for restoring the state of your computer if you ever install an application that wreaks havoc on your system. Theoretically, every time you install a new application or drive, a new restore point is created, which is then used to restore the state of your PC to what it was before the installation. But a restore point may not always be created, so if you're about to install a new application that you fear may not be well behaved, it's a good idea to manually create a restore point. System Restore automatically creates a Restore Point once a day as well as whenever a significant system event occurs, such as installing a driver or a new program.

Oddly enough, Windows calls the feature both System Protection and System Restore. System Protection actually refers to the overall configuration screen for System Restore, and System Restore is the actual application that creates restore points and performs system restorations.

## Task Manager                    \windows\system32\taskmgr.exe

Display currently running programs, background processes, and some performance statistics.

### To open

Ctrl-Alt-Delete → Start Task Manager

Right-click on empty portion of the Taskbar → Task Manager

Command Prompt → `taskmgr`

Keyboard shortcut: Ctrl-Shift-Esc

### Description

The Task Manager is an extremely useful tool, but you won't find it on the Start menu. In its simplest form, it displays all running applications, allowing you to close any that have crashed or stopped responding.

## Task Scheduler  \windows\system32\taskschd.msc

Run a program or script at a specified time.

### To open

Control Panel → [System and Maintenance] → Schedule tasks

Command Prompt → **taskschd**

### Description

The Task Scheduler allows you to schedule any program or WSH script to run at a specified time or interval.

To create a new scheduled task, click Create Basic Task to open the Task Scheduler Wizard. You'll be prompted to do the following:

1. Type in a name for the task and its description.
2. Select a trigger (for example, at a specific day, when your computer starts, when you log on, when a specific event occurs, and so on). The trigger can also be a specific time of the day and day of the week.
3. Select an action that the Task Scheduler should take (for example, run a program, send an email, or display a message).

Click Finish, and you're done. The task will now run at the scheduled time.

## Windows Easy Transfer

Transfers file, folders, and settings among PCs.

### To open

Control Panel → [System and Maintenance] → Welcome Center → Transfer Files and Settings

### Description

Windows Easy Transfer can transfer files, programs, and settings from a PC running Windows 2000, Windows XP, or Windows Vista to a PC running Windows Vista.

---

**TIP**

If you upgrade from a PC running Windows XP to Windows Vista, your files, settings, and programs will be transferred automatically.

---

You can use Windows Easy Transfer to transfer files and program settings from a computer running Windows 2000, Windows XP, or Windows Vista to another computer running Windows Vista. Start Windows Easy Transfer on the computer running Windows Vista, and then follow the instructions.

## Startup Repair

Fixes problems that can stop Windows from starting properly, such as missing or damaged files.

### To open

Insert the Windows installation disk into your PC, restart the computer, and click "View system recovery options." After typing in a username and password of an account on the computer, click Startup Repair.

### Description

If you can't start Windows properly, this utility scans your system and automatically tries to fix the problem. In some instances, a computer manufacturer will install Startup Repair on your hard disk. If so, you can run it not only from the Windows installation disk, but also from the Windows Advanced Startup Options menu (Control Panel → [System and Maintenance] → System → Advanced system settings → Advanced tab, click Settings in Startup and Recovery).

## System Configuration Utility          \windows\System32\msconfig.exe

Selectively enable or disable several startup options and get access to specialized tools to optimize performance, customize Windows Vista, and perform diagnostic/troubleshooting tasks.

---

**To open**

Command Prompt → `msconfig`

**Description**

The System Configuration Utility allows you to selectively enable or disable various settings that affect system startup, including the ability to stop specific programs and services from starting. In many instances, there is no other way to stop the programs or services from starting, so this utility is particularly useful. It can also help track down the causes of startup errors; use the utility to selectively disable programs or services from starting until you isolate the cause of the problems.

# Graphics and Multimedia

## Paint                                        \windows\system32\mspaint.exe

A rudimentary image editor, used to create and modify *.bmp*, *.jpg*, *.gif*, *.tif*, *.ico*, and *.png* image files.

**To open**

Start → All Programs → Accessories → Paint

Command Prompt → `mspaint`

**Description**

Paint is a basic image editor (often called a "paint program") capable of creating and modifying most Windows Bitmap (*.bmp*), Joint Photographic Experts Group (*.jpg*), Compuserve Graphics Interchange Format (*.gif*), Tagged Image File Format (*.tif*), and Portable Network Graphics (*.png*) image files. It can open icon (*.ico*) files but cannot save graphics in the *.ico* format. In essence, Paint is to image files as Notepad is to text files.

## Snipping Tool                          \windows\system32\SnippingTool.exe

Capture, annotate, and save screen captures.

## To open

Start → All Programs → Accessories → Snipping Tool

Command Prompt → **snippingtool**

## Description

The Snipping Tool, new to Windows Vista, lets you capture any portion of your screen, annotate that screen capture, and then copy it to the Clipboard or save it as a *.mht*, *.png*, *.gif*, or *.jpeg* file. When you run the Snipping Tool a small screen appears. The rest of your screen dims, and your cursor turns into a big + sign. If you want to snip a rectangular area, use the cursor to define the area. You can instead capture a freeform area, the entire screen, or a screen or object such as the Taskbar. To do that, click New in the Snipping Tool and make your choice of screen captures.

## Windows DVD Maker          *\Program Files\Movie Maker\DVDMaker.exe*

Create DVDs that you can watch on a TV.

## To open

Start → All Programs → Windows DVD Maker

Command Prompt → **dvdmaker**

## Description

Windows DVD Maker is a simple program for creating DVDs that you can play on a TV. It features a wizard-style interface and walks you through two screens to create a DVD.

## Windows Media Center          *C:\Windows\ehome\ehshell.exe*

Play and record media of all types, including TV.

## To open

Start → All Programs → Windows Media Center

Command Prompt → **ehshell** (only when you're in *C:\Windows\ ehome\*)

## Description

The Windows Media Center, previously available only in a special edition of Windows XP, ships with every copy of Windows Vista Home Premium and Windows Vista Ultimate. It uses an interface unlike any other program built into Windows, and it dispenses with menus, toolbars, and the usual screen elements you've grown used to in Windows; you instead navigate and choose features by using your mouse or arrow keys, or if you have one, a remote control. In fact, it looks more like it's been designed to be used with a remote control, rather than the keyboard.

Microsoft has been trying to make the Windows Media Center the center of home entertainment systems, and it has been designed to connect to TVs. Because it is supposed to have its place in the living room and has been designed to be accessed via remote control, it's simple and intuitive to use, so there's no need to delve into its general use in any great detail here.

The Windows Media Center interface is self-explanatory. Scroll to the kind of media you want to watch or record (Pictures & Videos, Music, TV & Movies, and so on) and select Program Library, or Recorded TV, to view a library of all the media in that category. Then select it to view it. The Windows Media Center uses the familiar VCR-like controls along the bottom of the screen (e.g., Play, Stop, etc.) to control your playing. You can also watch TV and play DVDs.

---

## Windows Media Player *C:\Program Files\Windows Media Player\wmplayer.exe*

Play back a wide variety of video and audio media files, such as *.mpg* movies, *.mp3* songs, *.wma* Windows media songs, audio CD tracks, *.dvr-ms* recorded TV shows, media files, and other streaming media.

### To open

Start → All Programs → Windows Media Player

Double-click on any associated media file.

Command Prompt → **wmplayer** (note: you have to be in *C:\ Program Files\Windows Media Player* to run it from the command prompt)

---

## Description

Windows Media Player is the default application used to open and play most of the types of video and audio media supported by Windows Vista. You can open Windows Media Player from the Start menu, as well as by double-clicking on a supported media file or clicking on a link in a web page to open that video or audio clip and play it. The program isn't configured or enabled until you launch it for the first time, at which point a simple configuration screen will appear.

Basic operation of Windows Media Player is fairly straightforward, with the standard VCR-like controls along the bottom of the screen (e.g., Play, Stop, etc.), the current view of your media or operations in the large, middle part of the screen, and navigation on the left part of the screen. This basic view, however, changes according to your current activity.

## Windows Movie Maker          *\program files\movie maker\moviemk.exe*

Capture and edit video, and create video clips.

### To open

Start → All Programs → Windows Movie Maker

Command Prompt → `moviemk` (you must be in the *movie maker* subdirectory to run this)

### Description

Windows Movie Maker has been significantly beefed up from its Windows XP incarnation, and it is now a full-featured program for creating videos. The Windows XP and Windows Vista versions of it have become popular for creating videos uploaded to video-sharing sites such as YouTube (*http://www.youtube.com*).

## Windows Photo Gallery          *\program files\Windows Photo Gallery\*
*WindowsPhotoGallery.exe*

Organize, view, and edit pictures and video clips.

## To open

Start → All Programs → Windows Photo Gallery

Command Prompt → **windowsphotogallery** (you must be in the *Windows Photo Gallery* subdirectory to run this)

## Description

Windows Photo Gallery is an organizational, viewing, and editing tool for handling digital pictures and video clips. It won't replace more powerful editing programs, but for most basic tasks such as viewing and organizing your clips, as well as for basic photo-editing tasks such as eliminating red eye, it's perfectly serviceable.

# CHAPTER 4

# Registry Tweaks

The Windows Registry is a database of settings used by Windows Vista and the individual applications that run on it. Knowing how to access and modify the Registry effectively is important for troubleshooting, customizing, and unlocking hidden features in Windows Vista.

## Registry Editor Crash Course

Although the Registry is stored in multiple files on your hard disk, it is represented by a single, logical, hierarchical structure, similar to the folders on your hard disk. The Registry Editor (Regedit.exe) is included with Windows Vista to enable you to view and manually edit the contents of the Registry.

When you open the Registry Editor, you'll see a window divided into two panes: the left side shows a tree with keys (represented as folders), and the right side shows the contents (values) stored in the currently selected key.

Editing the Registry generally involves navigating down through branches to a particular key and then modifying an existing value or creating a new key or value. You can modify the contents of any value by double-clicking it.

To add a new key or value, select New from the Edit menu, select what you want to add, and then type a name. You can delete a key or value by clicking on it and pressing the Del key or by right-clicking on it and selecting Delete. You can also rename any existing value and almost any key with the same methods used to rename files in Explorer: right-click on an object and click Rename, click on it twice (slowly), or just highlight it and press the F2 key. Renaming a key or value is a safe alternative to deleting.

---

**WARNING**

Although most Registry settings are entirely benign, you can irrevocably disable certain components of Windows Vista—or even prevent Windows from starting—if you don't exercise some caution. You can limit the risk by creating Registry patches (backups) of keys before you modify their contents by going to File ▸ Export. Better yet, a complete system backup will ensure that even the most severe mistakes are recoverable.

---

Similar to Explorer, though, is the notion of a *path*. A Registry path is a location in the Registry described by the series of nested keys in which a setting is located. For example, if a particular value is in the Microsoft key under SOFTWARE, which is under HKEY_LOCAL_MACHINE, the Registry path is HKEY_LOCAL_MACHINE\SOFTWARE\Microsoft.

# Registry Structure

The Registry is enormous and complex; a full Registry might easily contain 15,000 keys and 35,000 values. Entire books have been written about it, and I can't do it justice here. The purpose of this section is to arm you with a basic understanding of how the Registry is organized, not to document individual values in detail or suggest changes you might want to make with the Registry Editor.

The top level of the Registry is organized into five main *root* branches. By convention, the built-in top-level keys are always shown in all caps, even though the keys in the Registry are not case-sensitive. (For example, HKEY_CURRENT_USER\

SOFTWARE\MICROSOFT\Windows is identical to HKEY_CURRENT_ USER\Software\Microsoft\Windows.) Their purposes and contents are listed in the following summaries. Note that the root keys are sometimes abbreviated for convenience in documentation (although never in practice); these abbreviations are shown in parentheses. Subsequent sections discuss the contents of the root keys in more detail.

HKEY_CLASSES_ROOT (HKCR)

Contains file types, filename extensions, URL protocol prefixes, and registered classes. You can think of the information in this branch as the "glue" that binds Windows with the applications and documents that run on it. It is critical to drag-and-drop operations, context menus, double-clicking, and many other familiar user interface semantics. The actions defined here tell Windows how to react to every file type available on the system.

This entire branch is a mirror (or symbolic link) of HKEY_ LOCAL_MACHINE\SOFTWARE\Classes, provided as a root key purely for convenience.

HKEY_CURRENT_USER (HKCU)

Contains user-specific settings for the currently logged-in user. This entire branch is a mirror (or symbolic link) of one of the subkeys of HKEY_USERS (discussed shortly). This allows Windows and all applications to access and store information for the current user without having to determine which user is currently logged in.

An application that keeps information on a per-user basis should store its data in HKEY_CURRENT_USER\Software and put information that applies to all users of the application in HKEY_LOCAL_MACHINE\SOFTWARE. However, what Windows applications consider user-specific and what applies for all users on the machine is somewhat arbitrary. Like many aspects of Windows, the Registry provides a mechanism for applications to store configuration data, but it does little to enforce any policies about how and where that data will actually be stored.

---

HKEY_LOCAL_MACHINE (HKLM)

Contains information about hardware and software on the machine that is not specific to the current user.

HKEY_USERS (HKU)

Stores underlying user data from which HKEY_CURRENT_USER is drawn. Although several keys will often appear here, only one of them will ever be the active branch. See the discussion of HKEY_USERS, later in this chapter, for details.

HKEY_CURRENT_CONFIG (HKCC)

Contains hardware configuration settings for the currently loaded hardware profile. This branch works similarly to HKEY_CURRENT_USER in that it is merely a mirror (or symbolic link) of another key. In this case, the source is HKEY_LOCAL_MACHINE\SYSTEM\CurrentControlSet\Hardware Profiles\XXXX, in which XXXX is a key representing the numeric value of the hardware profile currently in use. On a system with only a single hardware profile, its value will most likely be 0001.

# Value Types

Values are where Registry data is actually stored (as opposed to keys, which are simply used to organize values). The Registry contains several types of values, each appropriate to the type of data it is intended to hold. There are six primary types of values that are displayed and modified in the Registry Editor:

*String values* (REG_SZ)

String values contain strings of characters, more commonly known as text. Most values discussed in this book are string values; they're the easiest to edit and are usually in plain English. In addition to standard strings, there are two far less common string variants, used for special purposes:

*Multistring values* (REG_MULTI_SZ)

> Contain several strings (usually representing a list of some sort), concatenated (glued) together and separated by null characters (ASCII code 00). The dialog used to modify these values is the same as for binary values. Note that the individual characters in REG_MULTI_SZ keys are also separated by null characters, so you'll actually see three null characters in a row between multiple strings.

*Expandable string values* (REG_EXPAND_SZ)

> Contain special variables into which Windows substitutes information before delivering to the owning application. For example, an expanded string value intended to point to a sound file may contain %SystemRoot%\media\startup.wav. When Windows reads this value from the Registry, it substitutes the full Windows path for the variable, %SystemRoot%; the resulting data then becomes (depending on where Windows is installed) c:\windows\media\startup.wav. This way, the value data is correct regardless of the location of the Windows folder.

*Binary values* (REG_BINARY)

> Similarly to string values, binary values hold strings of characters. The difference is the way the data is entered. Instead of a standard text box, binary data is entered with hexadecimal codes in an interface commonly known as a *hex editor*. Each individual character is specified by a two-digit number in base 16 (e.g., 6E is 110 in base 10), which allows characters not found on the keyboard to be entered. Note that you can type hex codes on the left or normal ASCII characters on the right, depending on where you click with the mouse.

> Note that hex values stored in binary Registry values are displayed in a somewhat unconventional format, in which the lowest-order digits appear first, followed by the next-higher pair of digits, and so on. In other words,

the digits in a binary value are paired and their order reversed: the hex value 1B3 thus needs to be entered as B3 01. If you want to convert a binary value shown in the Registry Editor to decimal, you'll have to reverse this notation. For example, to find the decimal equivalent of 47 00 65 6e, set the Windows Calculator to hexadecimal mode and enter 6e650047, and then switch to decimal mode to display the decimal equivalent, 1,852,112,967.

Binary values are often not represented by plain English and, therefore, should be left unchanged unless you either understand the contents or are instructed to change them by a solution in this book.

*DWORD values* (REG_DWORD)

Essentially, a DWORD is a number. Often, the contents of a DWORD value are easily understood, such as 0 for no and 1 for yes, or 60 for the number of seconds in some timeout setting. A DWORD value is used only where numerical digits are allowed; string and binary types allow anything.

---

### WARNING

In some circumstances, the particular number entered into a DWORD value is actually made up of several components, called *bytes*. The REG_DWORD_BIGENDIAN type is a variant of the DWORD type, where the bytes are in a different order. Unless you're a programmer, you'll want to stay away from these types of DWORD values.

---

The DWORD format, like the binary type, is a hexadecimal number, but this time in a more conventional representation. The leading 0x is a standard programmer's notation for a hex value, and the number is properly read from left to right. The equivalent decimal value is shown in parentheses following the hex value. What's more, when you edit a DWORD value, the edit dialog box gives you a choice of entering the new value in decimal or hex notation.

Even if you're not a programmer, you can figure out hexadecimal values pretty easily with the Windows Calculator (*calc.exe*). Just enter the number you want to convert and click the Hex radio button to see the hexadecimal equivalent; 435 decimal is equal to 1B3 hex.

---

**TIP**

If you aren't sure about the meaning of a specific Registry value, don't be afraid to experiment. Experimenting might include editing a value with the Registry Editor, but it might be easier or safer to work from the other end: open the application whose data is stored there (e.g., a Control Panel applet), change a setting, and watch how the Registry data changes. In this way, you can derive the meaning of many binary-encoded values. Note that although the Registry data will often change immediately, you may need to press F5 (Refresh) to force the Registry Editor to display the newly affected data. It's a good idea, though, to make a backup copy of a Registry key before making any changes.

---

*QWORD values* (REG_QWORD)
  This is much like a DWORD value, with one difference: it is a 64-bit value, rather than a 32-bit value like DWORD.

# Registry Protection in Windows Vista

Many of the changes made in Windows Vista have to do with safety and security, and with ensuring that the operating system doesn't accidentally become damaged. Toward that end, in Windows Vista, only accounts with administrator privileges can make changes to the Registry. This affects not just editing the Registry directly, but also taking an action that will change the Registry, such as installing software.

So, what happens when a standard user wants to edit the Registry or make a change that affects the Registry? Windows Vista handles that in several ways:

- When a standard user tries to run the Registry Editor, User Account Control (UAC) springs into action, asking for an administrator password. If one is provided, the Registry Editor can be used and changes made. If none is provided, the Registry Editor will not be allowed to run, and no changes will be made.

- When a standard user installs software, UAC will ask for an administrator password. If the user provides one, the software will make the appropriate changes to the *%SystemRoot%* and *%ProgramFiles%* folders and to the Registry.

If a legacy application fails to work correctly with UAC, Vista will use a new feature called *file and Registry virtualization*. This will create virtual *%SystemRoot%* and *%ProgramFiles%* folders, and a virtual HKEY_LOCAL_MACHINE Registry entry. These virtual folders and entry are stored with the user's files. So the Registry itself—as well as the *%SystemRoot%* and *%ProgramFiles%* folders—are not altered in any way, so system files and the Registry are protected.

# Registry Tweaks

Armed with your new understanding of the Windows Vista Registry, you're no doubt ready to get in there and start exploring. Hopefully, this chapter has provided the "lay of the land" you need to get and keep your bearings in the otherwise confusing wilderness of the Registry. Although I don't have the kind of room in this book that it takes to make you an expert, I would like to send you on your way by pointing out some interesting landmarks—in other words, five cool changes you can make in your own Registry.

# Open a Command Prompt from the Right-Click Menu

The command prompt is useful for a variety of down-and-dirty tasks, such as mass-deleting or renaming files. But if you find yourself frequently switching back and forth between Windows Explorer and the command prompt, there's help—you can easily open a command prompt using the right-click menu.

For example, let's say you want to open the command prompt at the folder that's your current location. Normally, that takes two steps: first open a command prompt, and then navigate to your current folder. However, there's a quicker way: add an option to the right-click context menu that will open a command prompt at your current folder. For example, if you were to right-click on the *C:\My Stuff* folder, you could then choose to open a command prompt at *C:\My Stuff*.

In the Registry Editor, go to `HKEY_LOCAL_MACHINE/Software/Classes/Folder/Shell`. Create a new key called `Command Prompt`. For the default value, enter whatever text you want to appear when you right-click on a folder—for example, **Open Command Prompt**. Create a new key beneath the `Command Prompt` key called `Command`. Set the default value to `Cmd.exe /k pushd %L`. That value will launch *Cmd.exe*, which is the Windows Vista command prompt. The `/k` switch puts the prompt into interactive mode—that is, it lets you issue commands from the command prompt; the command prompt isn't being used to issue only a single command and then exit. The `pushd` command stores the name of the current directory, and the `%L` uses the name of that stored directory to start the command prompt at it. Exit the Registry. The new menu option will show up immediately. Note that it won't appear when you right-click on a file—it shows up only when you right-click on a folder.

## Change the Ribbons Screensaver

Inexplicably, Windows Vista screensavers such as the Ribbon screensaver don't allow you to change how they work—for example, to change the number or width of the ribbons. But you can change their options, using the Registry. Here's how to change the Ribbons screensaver to make it use a larger number of ribbons, and make each ribbon much thinner.

In the Registry Editor, go to:

```
HKEY_CURRENT_USER\Software\Microsoft\Windows\
CurrentVersion\Screensavers\Ribbons
```

Create a new DWORD called `NumRibbons` and give it the hexadecimal value of 00000100. Next, create a new DWORD called `RibbonWidth` and give it the hexadecimal value of 3c23d70a0. Exit the Registry. The Ribbons screensaver will now have the new settings. To restore the old settings, delete the DWORDs.

## Registry Editor Remembers Where You Were

Each time you open the Registry Editor, it automatically expands the branch you had open the last time the Registry Editor was used, but no others. So, if you find yourself repeatedly adjusting a particular setting and then closing the Registry Editor (such as when implementing the preceding tip), make sure the relevant key is highlighted just before the Registry Editor is closed, and that key will be opened next time as well.

Note also the Favorites menu, which works very much like the one in Internet Explorer, allowing you to bookmark frequently accessed Registry keys. Although it's useful, I find the existence of such a feature in a troubleshooting tool like the Registry Editor to be more than a little eerie.

## Change the Registered Users and Company Names for Windows Vista

When Windows Vista is installed, a user and company name are entered. Unfortunately, there is no convenient way to change this information after installation. Surprise—you can do it in the Registry! Just go to:

```
HKEY_LOCAL_MACHINE\Software\Microsoft\Windows NT\
CurrentVersion
```

RegisteredOwner and RegisteredOrganization are the values you need, and you can change both to whatever you'd like. You may notice that the Registry key containing these values is in the Windows NT branch, rather than the more commonly used Windows branch. Don't worry, both branches are used in Windows Vista. The less-used Windows NT branch contains more advanced settings, mostly those that differentiate the Windows 9x and Windows NT lines of operating systems.

## Some Handy Registry Navigation Shortcuts

The Registry has thousands of keys and values, which makes finding a single key or value rather laborious. Luckily, there are a few alternatives that will greatly simplify this task.

First, you can simply search the Registry. Start by highlighting the key at the top of the tree through which you want to search, which instructs the Registry Editor to begin searching at the beginning of that key. (To search the entire Registry, highlight "Computer.") Then, use Edit → Find, type in what you're searching for, make sure that all the "Look at" options are checked, and click Find Next.

Another shortcut is to use the keyboard. Like Explorer, when you press a letter or number key, the Registry Editor will jump to the first entry that starts with that character. Furthermore, if you press several keys in succession, all of them will be used to spell the target item. For example, to navigate to:

```
HKEY_CLASSES_ROOT\CLSID\{20D04FE0-3AEA-1069-A2D8-
08002B30309D}
```

start by expanding the HKEY_CLASSES_ROOT key. Then, press C + L + S quickly in succession, and the Registry Editor will jump to the CLSID key. Next, expand that key by pressing the right-facing arrow, or by pressing the right arrow key, and press { + 2 + 0 (the first three characters of the key name, including the curly brace), and you'll be in the neighborhood of the target key in seconds.

# CHAPTER 5

# The Command Prompt

The premise of the Command Prompt is simple enough: commands are typed, one at a time, at a blinking cursor. The commands are then issued when you press the Enter key. After the command has completed, a new prompt is shown, allowing you to type additional commands. To run the Command Prompt, type **cmd** at Start Search or in the Address Bar of Windows Explorer.

Some commands are fairly rudimentary, requiring only that you type their names. Other commands are more involved and can require several options (sometimes called arguments or command-line parameters). For example, you use the del command (discussed later in this chapter) to delete one or more files; it requires that you specify the name of the file after the command, like this:

```
del /p myfile.txt
```

Here, *myfile.txt* is the filename to be deleted and /p is an extra option used to modify the behavior of del (it requires confirmation before it will delete each file). The fact that this usage is not limited to internal command prompt commands (such as del) is what makes the command line (but not necessarily the Command Prompt application) such an important part of Windows Vista's design. For example:

```
notepad myfile.txt
```

is what Windows executes behind the scenes, by default, when you double-click the *myfile.txt* icon in Explorer. Notepad is effectively a "command" here. If you type the filename of any existing file at the Command Prompt, it instructs Windows to launch that file. This works for applications, Windows Shortcuts, batch files, documents, or any other type of file; the only requirement is that the file be located in the current working directory (see "cd or chdir," later in this chapter) or in a folder specified in the path (also discussed later in this chapter).

# Wildcards, Pipes, and Redirection

In addition to the various command-line parameters used by each of the commands documented in this chapter (and the components documented in other places in this book), certain symbols used on the command line have special meaning. Table 5-1 shows these special symbols and what they do. You must use them in conjunction with other commands (they don't stand alone), and you can use them in the Command Prompt window, in Start → Run, and in an Address Bar.

*Table 5-1. Special symbols on the command line*

| Symbol | Description |
| --- | --- |
| * | Multiple-character wildcard, used to specify a group of files. |
| ? | Single-character wildcard, used to specify multiple files with more precision than *. |
| . | One dot represents the current directory; see "cd or chdir," later in this chapter. |
| .. | Two dots represent the parent directory; see "cd or chdir," later in this chapter. |
| \ | Separates directory names, drive letters, and filenames. By itself, \ represents the root directory of the current drive. |
| \\ | Indicates a network location, such as \\Joe-PC for a PC connected to your current network. |
| > | Redirects a command's text output into a file instead of the Console window; if that file exists, it will be overwritten. |
| >> | Appends a command's text output to the end of a file instead of the Console window. |

*Table 5-1. Special symbols on the command line (continued)*

| Symbol | Description |
| --- | --- |
| < | Directs the contents of a text file to a command's input; use with filter programs (such as sort) or in place of keyboard entry to automate interactive command-line applications. |
| \| | Redirects the output of a program or command to a second program or command (this is called a *pipe*). |

# Command Prompt Commands

## Attrib
\windows\system32\attrib.exe

Change or view the attributes of one or more files or folders.

### To open

Command Prompt → **attrib**

### Usage

```
attrib [+r|-r] [+a|-a] [+s|-s] [+h|-h] [filename] [/s [/d]]
```

### Description

Attrib allows you to change the file and folder attributes from the command line—settings otherwise available only in the Properties window of a file or folder. You can think of the attributes as switches, independently turned on or off for any file or group of files. The individual attributes are as follows:

R *(read-only)*
> Turn on the read-only attribute of a file or folder to protect it from accidental deletion or modification. If you attempt to delete a read-only file, Windows will prompt you before allowing you to delete it. Different applications handle read-only files in different ways; usually you will not be allowed to save your changes to the same filename.

A *(archive)*
> The archive attribute has no effect on how a file is used, but it is automatically turned on when a file is modified or created.

It is used primarily by backup software to determine which files have changed since a backup was last performed; most backup programs turn off the archive attribute on each file that is backed up.

S *(system)*

Files with the system attribute are typically used to boot the computer. There's little reason to modify a file with the system attribute, or to ever turn on or off the system attribute for any file. If you turn off the system attribute of an important file, it may stop the file from working.

H *(hidden)*

To hide any file or folder from plain view in Explorer or on the Desktop, turn on its hidden attribute.

## Examples

To hide a file in Explorer, right-click on it, select Properties, and turn on the hidden option. To hide the same file using the command line, type:

```
attrib +h filename
```

where *filename* is the full path- and filename of the file to change. To specify multiple files, include a wildcard, such as \*.\* (for all files) or \*.txt (for all files with the *.txt* filename extension). Note the use of the plus sign (+) to turn on an attribute; use the minus sign (–) to turn it off. For example, to turn off the hidden attribute and simultaneously turn on the archive attribute, type:

```
attrib -h +a filename
```

To display the attributes of a file or a group of files in Explorer, select Details from the View menu. Then, select Choose Details from the View menu and turn on the Attributes option. To display the attributes of a file or a group of files on the command line, type:

```
attrib filename
```

where *filename* is the full path- and filename(s) of the files you want to view. Omit *filename* to display the attributes of all the files in the current folder. If *filename* is not used, or if it contains wildcards (in other words, if the command is intended to act on more than one file), you can use the /s option to further include the contents of all subfolders of the current folder. The /d option instructs Attrib to act upon folders as well as files, but it has meaning only if you use it in conjunction with the /s parameter.

## cd or chdir

Display the name of, or change, the current working directory (folder).

### Usage

```
cd [/d] [directory]
chdir [/d] [directory]
```

### Description

With no arguments, cd displays the full pathname of the current directory. Given the pathname of an existing directory, it changes the current directory to the specified directory.

If *directory* is on a different drive (for example, if the current directory is *c:\dream* and you type **cd d:\nightmare**), the current working directory on that drive is changed, but the current working drive is not. To change the current drive, use the /d parameter, or simply type the letter followed by a colon, by itself, at the prompt (see the following examples).

Pathnames can be absolute (including the full path starting with the root) or relative to the current directory. A path can be optionally prefixed with a drive letter. The special path .. refers to the parent of the current directory.

### Examples

If the current drive is *C:*, make *c:\temp\wild* the current directory:

```
C:\>cd \temp\wild
C:\temp\wild>
```

Note how the current working directory is displayed in the prompt. If the current directory is *c:\temp*, all that is necessary is:

```
C:\temp>cd wild
C:\temp\wild>
```

Change to the parent directory:

```
C:\more\docs\misc>cd ..
C:\more\docs>
```

Change to the root directory of the current drive:

```
C:\Windows\Desktop\>cd \
C:\>
```

Change to another drive:

```
C:\>cd /d d:\
D:\>
```

or simply:

```
C:\>d:
D:\>
```

## cls

Clear the Command Prompt window and buffer, leaving only the Command Prompt and cursor.

### Description

Type **cls** at the prompt to clear the screen and the screen buffer, which is useful for privacy concerns or simply reducing clutter.

The difference between using cls and simply closing the current Command Prompt window and opening a new one is that your working environment (such as the current directory) is preserved with cls.

## copy

Copy one or more files to another location.

### Usage

```
copy source destination
copy [/a | /b] source [/a | /b] [+ source [/a | /b]
[+ ...]] [destination [/a | /b]] [/v] [/y | /-y]
[/d] [/z] [/n] [/l]
```

## Description

copy makes a complete copy of an existing file. If another file by the same name exists at *destination*, you will be asked whether you want to overwrite it.

Omit the destination to copy the specified files to the current working directory. If the file (or files) to be copied is in a different directory or on a different disk, you can omit the destination filename. The resulting copy or copies will have the same name as the original.

You can use the special device name con (or con:) in place of either the source (or destination) filename to copy from the keyboard to a file (or from a file to the screen).

copy accepts the following parameters and options:

/a    Specifies that the file to copy is in ASCII format.

/b    Specifies that the file to copy is a binary file.

/v    Verifies that new files are written successfully by comparing them with the originals.

/y    Suppresses prompting to confirm that you want to overwrite an existing destination file.

/-y   Enables prompting to confirm that you want to overwrite an existing destination file with the same name (default).

/d    Allows the new file to be created as a decrypted file (NTFS volumes only).

/l    When copying a symbolic link (see "mklink," later in this chapter), copies the file as a link rather than making a couple of the source file (the default behavior).

/n    Copies the file using the short filename that Vista generated for compatibility with DOS, old versions of Windows, and devices that can't support long filenames on their flash memory.

/z    Copies networked files in restartable mode. If the network connection is lost during copying (if the server goes offline and severs the connection, for example), /z will resume the copying after the connection is reestablished.

## Examples

Copy the file *temp.txt* from *C:\* to *d:\files* (all three examples do the same thing):

```
C:\>copy c:\temp.txt d:\files\temp.txt
C:\>copy c:\temp.txt d:\files
C:\>copy temp.txt d:\files
```

The third sample in the preceding code works here because the source file is located in the current directory. Here's another way to do it:

```
C:\>d:
D:\>cd \files
D:\files>copy c:\temp.txt
```

Copy all the files from the directory *d:\Cdsample\Images* to the current directory, giving the copies the same names as the originals:

```
C:\>copy d:\cdsample\images\*.*
C:\>copy d:\cdsample\images\*.* .
```

Copy the file *words.txt* in the current directory to *d:\files*, renaming it *morewords.txt*:

```
C:\>copy words.txt d:\files\morewords.txt
```

Copy all of the files in the current directory to *d:\files* (all three examples do the same thing):

```
C:\>copy *.* d:\files
C:\>copy .\*.* d:\files
C:\>copy . d:\files
```

## date

Display or set the system date.

### Usage

```
date [/t | date]
```

## Description

date is essentially a holdover from the very early days of DOS when the user was required to enter the system date and time every time the computer was started. Now it's essentially included as a way to set the date from the command line; the preferred method is to use Control Panel → [Clock, Language and Region] → Date and Time.

If you type **date** on the command line without an option, the current date setting is displayed and you are prompted for a new one. Press Enter to keep the same date.

date accepts the following options:

*date*
> Specifies the date. Use the *mm-dd*-[ *yy* ] *yy* format. Values for *yy* can be from 80 through 99; values for *yyyy* can be from 1980 through 8907. Separate month, day, and year with periods, hyphens, or slashes.

/t
> Displays the current date without prompting for a new one. You can use this if you need to append a timestamp to the end of a file, as in date /t >> logfile.txt.

## del or erase

Delete one or more files.

### Usage

```
del [/p] [/f] [/s] [/q] [/a:attributes] filename
erase [/p] [/f] [/s] [/q] [/a:attributes] filename
```

### Description

You use the del command to delete one or more files from the command line without sending them to the Recycle Bin.

The del options are:

*filename*
> Specifies the file(s) to delete. If you do not specify the drive or path, the file is assumed to be in the current directory. You can use standard * and ? wildcards to specify the files to delete.

/p   Prompts for confirmation before deleting each file.

/f   Forces deletion of read-only files.

/s   Deletes specified files in all subdirectories (when using wildcards).

/q   Quiet mode; do not prompt if *filename* is *.*.

/a:*attributes*
    Selects files to delete based on attributes (read-only, hidden, system, or archive). See "Attrib," earlier in this chapter, for more information on attributes.

## Examples

Delete the file *myfile.txt* in the current directory:

    C:\>del myfile.txt

Delete the file *myfile.txt* in the *c:\files* directory:

    C:\>del c:\files\myfile.txt

Delete all files with the pattern *myfile.** (e.g., *myfile.doc*, *myfile.txt*, etc.) in the current directory, but prompt for each deletion:

    C:\>del c:\files\myfile.* /p

## dir

Display a list of files and subdirectories in a directory (folder).

## Usage

    dir [filename] [/b] [/c] [/d] [/l] [/n] [/p] [/q] [/s]
    [/w] [/x] [/4] [/a:attributes] [/o:sortorder]
    [/t:timefield]

## Description

Without any options, dir displays the disk's volume label and serial number, a list of all files and subdirectories (except hidden and system files) in the current directory, file/directory size, date/time of last modification, the long filename, the total number of files listed, their cumulative size, and the free space (in bytes) remaining on the disk.

If you specify one or more file or directory names (optionally including drive and path, or the full UNC path to a shared directory), information for only those files or directories will be listed.

You can use wildcards (* and ?) to display a subset of files and subdirectories in a given location.

dir accepts the following options:

*/a:attributes*
> Displays only files with/without specified attributes (using - as a prefix specifies "not," and a colon between the option and attribute is optional). See "Attrib," earlier in this chapter, for more information on attributes.

/b   Use bare format (no heading information or summary). Use with /s to list all files in the current directory and subdirectories.

/c   Displays the thousand separator in file sizes. This is the default; use /-c to disable display of the separator.

/d   Same as /w, except files are sorted vertically.

/l   Use lowercase.

/n   Lists files in a Unix-like display, where filenames are shown on the right. This is the default view.

*/o:sortorder*
> Lists files in sorted order (using - as a prefix reverses the order, and a colon between the option and attribute is optional):

> d   By date and time (earliest first)

> e   By extension (sorted alphabetically)

> g   Group directories first

> n   By name (sorted alphabetically)

> s   By size (smallest first)

/p   Pauses after each screenful of information; press any key to continue.

/q   Displays the owner of each file.

/s   Includes all files in all subdirectories, in addition to those in the current directory.

/t:*timefield*

Controls which time is used when sorting:

c Created

a Last accessed

w Last modified (written)

/w Wide list format. File- and directory names are listed in columns and sorted horizontally. The actual number of columns varies based on the length of the longest filename and the screen width. Use /d instead to sort vertically.

/x Include the "short" 8.3 versions of long filenames. For example, *Sam's File.txt* has an alternate filename, *samsfi~1.txt*, to maintain compatibility with older applications.

/4 Display the listed years as four digits. By default, two-digit years are displayed.

### Examples

Display all files in the current directory:

    C:\>dir

Display all files in the current directory that end with the *.txt* extension:

    C:\>dir *.txt

Display all files, listing years in four digits and pausing for each screenful:

    C:\>dir /4 /p

Display all files, sorted by date and time, latest first:

    C:\>dir /o-d

Display only directories:

    C:\>dir /ad

List all files on disk, sorted by size, and store output in the file *allfiles.txt*:

    C:\>dir \ /s /os > allfiles.txt

List the contents of the shared folder *cdrom* on machine *bubba*:

    C:\>dir \\bubba\cdrom

## echo

Display a string of text; turn command echoing on or off.

### Usage

```
echo [on | off | message]
```

### Description

echo is typically used with other commands or in a batch file to display text on the screen. It's also used to control command echoing from batch files.

You can use the following options with echo:

on | off

> By default, each command in a batch file is echoed to the screen as it is executed; echo on and echo off toggle this feature. To turn echoing off without displaying the echo off command, use @echo off. The @ symbol in front of any command in a batch file prevents the line from being displayed.

message

> Types the message you'd like displayed to the console (screen).

### Examples

To display an ordinary message, use the following:

```
echo Hello World!
```

To display a blank line, use one of the following (both are equivalent):

```
echo.
echo,
```

(Note the absence of the space between the echo command and the punctuation; you can also use a colon, semicolon, square brackets, backslash, or forward slash.)

One handy use of echo is to answer y to a confirmation prompt such as the one del issues when asked to delete all the files in a

---

directory. For example, if you wanted to clear out the contents of the \temp directory from a batch file, you could use the following command:

```
echo y | del c:\temp\*.*
```

or even:

```
echo y | if exists c:\temp\*.* del c:\temp\*.*
```

This construct works because the pipe character takes the output of the first command and inserts it as the input to the second.

You can use echo to announce the success or failure of a condition tested in a batch file:

```
if exist *.rpt echo The report has arrived.
```

It's a good idea to give users usage or error information in the event that they don't supply proper arguments to a batch file. You can do that as follows:

```
@echo off
if (%1) == ( ) goto usage
. . .
goto end
:usage
echo You must supply a filename.
:end
```

---

## find
\Windows\System32\find.exe

Search in one or more files for text.

### Usage

```
find [/v] [/c] [/n] [/i] [/offline] "string"
[filename[ ...]]
```

### Description

After searching the specified files, find displays any lines of text that contain the string you've specified for your search. find is useful for searching for specific words (strings) in files.

The find options are:

"string"
> The text to look for, enclosed in quotation marks.

*filename*
> The file(s) in which to search. Wildcards (*, ?) are supported, and you can specify multiple filenames as long as you separate them with commas. If *filename* is omitted, find searches text typed at the prompt or piped from another command via the pipe character (|), as described in "Wildcards, Pipes, and Redirection," earlier in this chapter.

/c   Displays only the count of lines containing the string.

/i   Ignores the case of characters when searching for the string.

/n   Displays line numbers with the displayed lines.

/v   Displays all lines not containing the specified string.

*/offline*
> Includes files with the offline attribute set (that otherwise would be skipped).

### Examples

Search for *redflag* in *myemployees.txt*:

```
C:\>find "redflag" myemployees.txt
```

Count occurrences of the word *deceased* in *myemployees.txt*:

```
C:\>find /c "deceased" myemployees.txt
```

Search the current directory for the string "cls" in all *.bat* files and store the result in the file *cls.txt* (note that >> rather than > is necessary when redirecting the output of a for loop):

```
C:\>for  %f in (*.bat) do find "cls" %f >> cls.txt
```

## md or mkdir

Create a new directory (folder).

### Usage

```
md [drive:]path
mkdir [drive:]path
```

## Description

Windows Vista, like its predecessors, uses a hierarchical directory structure to organize its filesystem. On any physical disk, the filesystem begins with the root directory, signified by a lone backslash.

md and mkdir accept the following option:

*[drive:]path*
    Specifies the directory to create.

## Examples

Create a subdirectory named *harry* in the current directory:

    C:\tom\dick>**md harry**

Create a new directory called *newdir* under the *c:\olddir* directory:

    C:\>**md c:\olddir\newdir**

If *c:\olddir* doesn't exist, it will be created as well.

Create two new directories, *c:\rolling* and *c:\stones*:

    C:\>**md rolling stones**

Create a single new directory, *c:\rolling stones*:

    C:\>**md "rolling stones"**

(Enclose directory names in quotation marks to accommodate spaces.)

---

## mklink

Create a link to another file or directory.

### Usage

    mklink [[/d] | [/h] | [/j]] *link target*

### Description

mklink is used to create a Unix-style link to another file or directory; that link can be used just as if it were the original file or directory. When you create a *symbolic* link to a file, that file will show up in Windows Explorer as a shortcut, and if you use the

---

command line to get a directory listing, it will be listed as a `<SYMLINK>` instead of as `<DIR>`, and you'll see the symbolic link followed by the real file. For example, if you create a symbolic link called *newone* to the file *test*, here's what you would see:

```
<SYMLINK>        newone [c:\test]
```

The mklink options are:

/d   Creates a symbolic link (the default). Use /j for directories.

/h   Creates a hard link instead of a symbolic link. You will not see SYMLINK in the *dir* listing, because a hard link is a first-class filename. Creating a hard link to an existing file adds another filename, and the file is not deleted until you delete the last hard link to it.

/j   Creates a directory junction. You will see JUNCTION in the *dir* listing instead of SYMLINK.

*link*
> Specifies the new symbolic link name.

*target*
> Specifies the path (relative or absolute) that the new link refers to.

---

### move

Specifies the path (relative or absolute) that the new link refers to.

Move files and directories from one location to another.

#### Usage

```
move [/y | /-y] filename[,...] destination
```

#### Description

move works like copy, except that the source is deleted after the copy is complete. *filename* can be a single file, a group of files (separated by commas), or a single file specification with wildcards.

The move options are:

*filename*
> Specify the location and name(s) of the file or files you want to move. Wildcards (*, ?) are supported.

*destination*
> Specify the new location of the file. The destination parameter can consist of a drive, a directory name, or a combination of the two. When moving one file, *destination* may include a new name for the file. If you include the new filename but omit the drive or directory name, move effectively renames the file.

/y   Suppress prompting to confirm creation of a directory or overwriting of the destination. This is the default when move is used in a batch file.

/-y
> Cause prompting to confirm creation of a directory or overwriting of the destination. This is the default when move is used from the command line.

### Examples

Move *myfile.txt* from the current directory to *d:\files*:

```
C:\>move myfile.txt d:\files\
```

Same, but rename the file to *newfile.txt*:

```
C:\>move myfile.txt d:\files\newfile.txt
```

Change the name of the directory *d:\files* to *d:\myfiles*:

```
D:\>move d:\files myfiles
```

## path

Set or display the command search path.

### Usage

```
path [path1][;path2][;path3][;...]
```

### Description

When you type an executable filename at the Command Prompt (as opposed to a command built into the Command Prompt), Windows starts by looking in the current directory for a file that matches. If no matching file is found, Windows then looks in a series of other folders, which are known collectively as the path or the *command search path*.

The path statement is used to define additional directories to be included while searching for files. The path consists of a series of absolute directory pathnames, separated by semicolons. No spaces should follow each semicolon, and there should be no semicolon at the end of the statement. If no drive letter is specified, all pathnames are assumed to be on the current directory's drive.

Type **path** without any arguments to display the current command search path. The default path in Windows Vista is c:\windows\system32;c:\windows;c:\windows\system32\wbem.

When you type the name of a command, DOS looks first in the current directory and then in each successive directory specified in the path. Within each directory, it will look for executable files by their extension in the following order: *.com*, *.exe*, *.bat*, *.cmd*. Windows searches your path for certain other file types (i.e., *.dll* or *.ocx*) as well, although most cannot be executed from the command line.

### Examples

Specify the directories *c:\Stuff* and *d:\Tools* in the path:

```
C:\>path c:\stuff;d:\tools
```

However, this will replace the path with these two folders. To add these folders to the existing path, type the following:

```
C:\>path %path%;c:\stuff;d:\tools
```

## prompt

Change the appearance of the prompt.

## Usage

```
prompt [text]
```

## Description

Type **prompt** by itself (without *text*) to reset the prompt to its default setting.

The prompt options are:

*text*

> Specifies a new command prompt. *text* can contain normal characters and the following special codes:

> $_ Carriage return and linefeed

> $$ Dollar sign ($)

> $a Ampersand (&)

> $b Pipe (|)

> $c Left parenthesis (()

> $d Current date

> $e Escape character (ASCII code 27), used to provide extended formatting

> $f Right parenthesis ())

> $g Greater-than sign (>), commonly known as the caret

> $h Backspace (erases preceding character)

> $l Less-than sign (<)

> $n Current drive

> $p Current drive and path

> $q Equals sign (=)

> $s Space

> $t Current time

> $v Windows version number

## Examples

Specify the current drive and directory followed by the greater-than sign (>), the default prompt in Windows Vista:

```
C:\>prompt $p$g
```

Specify the drive and directory on one line and the date, followed by the greater-than sign (>), on another:

```
C:\>prompt $p$_$d$g
```

Specify the drive only, followed by the greater-than sign (>), which was the default prompt on early versions of DOS:

```
C:\>prompt $n$g
```

## query

Find out information about sessions, processes, and users.

### Usage

```
query process | session | termserver | user
```

### Description

The query options are:

process
> Lists the currently running processes, including filenames, and associated usernames

session
> Lists the current sessions, including their IDs and associated usernames

termserver
> Lists the currently running terminal servers

user
> Lists information about logged-in users, including the time they logged on, their amount of idle time, their session name, and their session ID

## quser

Displays information about users currently logged on to the system. (Not available in the Home edition.)

### Usage

```
quser username sessionname sessionid
```

## Description

quser displays information about currently logged-on users. It displays when the user logged on, whether the user is active, and the current time, the username, the session name, the session ID, and the amount of idle time for the user. (To find the session ID, use the query command. See the preceding section, "query.") You can use the following commands with quser:

username
> Identifies the username of the user for whom you want to display information

sessionname
> Displays the session name (for example, console) of the user for whom you want to display information

sessionid
> Displays the session ID (for example, 2) of the user for whom you want to display information

## Examples

Display information about the user preston:

```
quser preston
```

Display information about the user with the session name console:

```
quser console
```

## rd or rmdir

Remove (delete) a directory.

## Usage

```
rd [/s] [/q] path
rmdir [/s] [/q] path
```

## Description

Unlike in Windows Explorer, files and folders are deleted differently; if you try to use del to delete a directory, it will simply delete all the files in the directory, but the directory itself will remain. You use rd to delete empty directories and, optionally, to delete directories and all of their contents.

rd accepts the following options:

*path*
> Specifies the directory to delete.

/s  Removes all files and subdirectories of the specified directory.

/q  Quiet mode; don't prompt when using /s.

### Examples

Delete the empty subdirectory called *newdir* located in the *c:\ olddir* directory:

```
C:\>rd c:\olddir\newdir
```

Delete the directory *Online Services* and all of its contents within the current directory, *c:\Program Files*:

```
C:\Program Files>rd /s "online services"
```

Note that you must use quotes with rd for folders with spaces in their names.

---

## ren or rename

Rename a file or directory.

### Usage

```
ren [filename1] [filename2]
rename [filename1] [filename2]
```

### Description

Use ren to rename any file or directory. Unlike in Windows Explorer, though, ren is capable of renaming several files at once (via the wildcards * and ?).

The ren options are:

[*filename1*]
> The name of the existing file or directory

[*filename2*]
> The new name to assign to the file or directory

---

## Examples

Rename *myfile.txt* to *file.txt*:

```
C:\>rename myfile.txt file.txt
```

Rename *chap 5.doc* to *sect 5.doc* (the following two methods are identical):

```
C:\>ren "chap 5.doc" "sect 5.doc"
C:\>ren chap?5.doc sect?5.doc
```

Each of these examples represents different ways to rename files with spaces in their names. In addition to the standard quotation marks, in certain circumstances you can use wildcards to avoid the space problem. Here, both *chap 5.doc* and *sect 5.doc* have spaces in the fifth character position, so you can use the single wildcard character (?).

Rename the files *chap1.doc*, *chap2.doc*, etc., to *revchap1.doc*, *revchap2.doc*, etc.:

```
C:\>ren chap*.doc revchap*.doc
```

ren can be a convenient way to rename the filename extensions of several files at once, as well:

```
C:\>ren *.txt *.rtf
C:\>ren *.htm *.html
C:\>ren *.mpeg *.mpg
```

## robocopy

A powerful, flexible tool for copying files.

### Usage

```
robocopy source [drive:\path or \\server\share\path]
destination [drive:\path or \\server\share\path] [file
[file]...] /a /m /s /e /mov /move /lev:n /fat
```

### Description

robocopy stands for *Robust Copy for Windows*, and the name is apt. It is far more powerful than the copy and xcopy commands, and in fact, a full explication of all of its commands and uses would take up half this chapter. For details about its full usage, type **robocopy /?** to get help.

You can use the command to copy files not only on a PC, but also between PCs and servers, and between servers as well. It can use wildcards for file selection.

The following are some of the primary commands that you can use with robocopy:

/a   Copy only files with the Archive attribute set.

/m   Copy only files with the Archive attribute and reset it.

/s   Copy subdirectories, but not empty ones.

/e   Copy subdirectories, including empty ones.

/mov
:   Move files (delete from source after copying).

/move
:   Move files and directories (delete from source after copying).

/lev:*n*
:   Copy on the top *n* levels of the source directory tree.

/fat
:   Create destination files using 8.3 FAT filenames only.

/mir
:   Mirrors a complete directory tree. You also can use it with other commands, such as /b for copying files in backup mode, to copy only files that have been changed.

### Examples

Copy all *.xls* files from *C:\newbudget* to *F:\newbudget*, and use only 8.3 FAT filenames:

```
robocopy *.xls c:\newbudget f:\newbudget /fat
```

## set

Display, assign, or remove environment variables.

### Usage

```
set [variable[=[string]]]
set /p variable=[promptstring]
set /a expression
```

## Description

The *environment* is a small portion of memory devoted to the storage of a few values called environment variables. You use set to manipulate environment variables from the command line, but because the Command Prompt's environment is reset when its window is closed, the usefulness of set is fairly limited for interactive use, although you'll use it a lot in your own batch files.

To make more permanent changes to environment variables, go to Control Panel → [System and Maintenance] → System → Advanced system settings → Environment variables. The variables in the upper listing are for the current user and the variables in the lower listing apply to all users. Some environment variables, such as the Temp user variable, are assigned with respect to other variables, like this:

    %USERPROFILE%\AppData\Local\Temp

where %USERPROFILE% (note the percent signs [%] on both sides) signifies the USERPROFILE variable, which represents the path of the current user's home directory. See "path," earlier in this chapter, for another example of this usage.

In addition to providing a simple means of interapplication communication, environment variables are also useful for storing data used repeatedly in a batch file.

Type **set** without options to display all of the current environment variables. Type **set** with only a variable name (no equals sign or value) to display a list of all the variables whose prefix matches the name.

The set options are:

*variable*

> Specifies the variable name. When assigning a new variable, the case used is preserved. But when referencing, modifying, or deleting the variable, *variable* is case-insensitive. If *variable* is specified by itself, its value is displayed. If *variable* is specified by itself with an equals sign, the variable is assigned an empty value and deleted. *Variable* cannot contain the equals sign (=).

*string*

> Specifies a series of characters to assign to *variable*. As stated earlier, this can contain references to other variables when surrounded with preceding and trailing percent signs (%).

/p   Specifies that *variable* will be assigned by text input from the user, rather than *string*. As stated earlier, this can contain references to other variables with preceding and trailing percent signs (%).

*promptstring*
   The text prompt to display when using the /p option.

/a   Specifies that *expression* is a numerical expression to be evaluated. If used from the Command Prompt, set /a will display the final evaluated result of *expression*, even if you include an assignment operator (such as =) to assign a variable.

*expression*
   When used with the /a option, *expression* is a collection of symbols, numbers, and variables arranged so that it can be evaluated by set. The following symbols are recognized (in decreasing order of precedence):

   ( )  Parentheses for grouping

   ! ~ -  Unary operators (not, bitwise not, negative)

   */ %  Arithmetic operators (multiply, divide, modulus)

   +-   Arithmetic operators (add, subtract)

   << >>
      Logical shift

   &   Bitwise "and"

   ^   Bitwise "exclusive or"

   |   Bitwise "or"

   = *= /= %= += -= &= ^= |= <<= >>=
      Assignment

   '   Expression separator

   If you use /a with any of the bitwise or modulus operators, you need to enclose *expression* in quotes. Any non-numeric strings in *expression* are treated as environment variable names, and their values are converted to numbers during evaluation (zero is used for undefined variables); the percent signs (%) are not used here.

**Examples**

Set the variable dummy to the string not much:

```
C:\>set dummy=not much
```

Set the dircmd variable, which instructs the dir command (discussed earlier in this chapter) to sort directory listings by size, with the largest first:

```
C:\>set dircmd=/s /o-s
```

Append the directory *c:\mystuff* to the path (see "path," earlier in this chapter); note how the path variable is used on the right side of the equals sign so that its original contents aren't lost:

```
C:\>set path=%path%;c:\mystuff
```

Set the prompt (see "prompt," earlier in this chapter) to show the current time, followed by a right-angle bracket:

```
C:\>set prompt=$t>
```

Display the contents of the variable named dummy (both of the following statements are equivalent):

```
C:\>set dummy
C:\>echo %dummy%
```

You can also reference environment variables with other commands:

```
C:\>set workdir=C:\stuff\tim's draft
C:\>cd %workdir%
```

Here, the environment variable is used to store a long pathname for quick navigation to a frequently used directory.

Display the values of all variables that begin with the letter *H*:

```
C:\>set h
```

Clear the value of an environment variable, dummy:

```
C:\>set dummy=
```

Prompt the user to enter text to be inserted into the dummy variable. This is typically used in batch files (note that you have to put quotes around it, otherwise the > will be interpreted as the redirection operator):

```
C:\>set /p dummy="Enter text here >"
```

Evaluate an arithmetic expression (the two following expressions are not the same):

```
C:\>set /a 7+(3*4)
C:\>set /a (7+3)*4
```

The results of these two expressions, 19 and 40, respectively, will be displayed. To assign the result to a variable, type the following:

```
C:\>set /a dummy=7+(3*4)
```

Even though you're assigning the result variable, the result will still be displayed (unless set is executed from a batch file). To suppress the output, type this:

```
C:\>set /a dummy=7+(3*4) > nul
```

In addition to any custom environment variables you may use, Windows Vista recognizes the following variables (many of which are predefined):

ALLUSERSPROFILE
> The location of the All Users folder, usually *c:\Users\All Users*.

APPDATA
> The location of the Application Data folder, usually *c:\Users\ %USERNAME%\AppData\Roaming*.

COMMONPROGRAMFILES
> The location of the Common Files folder, usually *c:\Program Files\Common Files*.

COMPUTERNAME
> The network name of the computer, which you can set by going to Control Panel → [System and Maintenance] → See the name of this computer → Change settings.

COMSPEC
> The location of the Command Prompt application executable, *c:\Windows\system32\cmd.exe* by default.

COPYCMD
> Whether the copy, move, and xcopy commands should prompt for confirmation before overwriting a file. The default value is /-y. To stop the warning messages, set copycmd to /y.

---

**DIRCMD**

Specifies the default options for the dir command. For example, setting dircmd to /p will cause dir to always pause after displaying a screenful of output.

**ERRORLEVEL**

The return code of the last command run. A zero value (0) indicates success; anything else indicates failure.

**HOMEDRIVE**

The drive letter of the drive containing the current user's home directory, usually *c:*, used with HOMEPATH.

**HOMEPATH**

Along with HOMEDRIVE, the path of the current user's home directory, which is usually *\Users\%USERNAME%*.

**LOGONSERVER**

The name of the computer as seen by other computers on your network, usually the same as COMPUTERNAME preceded by two backslashes.

**NUMBER_OF_PROCESSORS**

The number of processors currently installed. In a multiprocessor or multicore system, it can be two, four, or more.

**OS**

Used to identify the operating system to some applications; for Windows XP, OS is set to Windows_NT. You may be able to "fool" an older program that is programmed not to run on an NT system by changing this variable temporarily.

**PATH**

The sequence of directories in which the command interpreter will look for commands to be interpreted.

**PATHEXT**

The filename extensions (file types) Windows will look for in the directories listed in the path. The default is *.COM*, *.EXE*, *.BAT*, *.CMD*, *.VBS*, *.VBE*, *.JS*, *.JSE*, *.WSF*, *.WSH*, and *.MSC*.

**PROCESSOR_ARCHITECTURE**

The type of processor; set to x86 for 32-bit Windows running on Intel-compatible processors (such as the Core 2 Duo or Athlon X2).

PROCESSOR_REVISION

A series of values the processor manufacturer uses to identify the processor.

PROGRAMFILES

The location of the Program Files folder, usually *c:\Program Files*.

PROMPT

The format of the command-line prompt, usually $P$G. See "prompt," earlier in this chapter, for details.

SESSIONNAME

The name of the current Command Prompt session, usually Console.

SYSTEMDRIVE

The drive letter of the drive containing Windows, usually *C:*.

SYSTEMROOT

The location of the Windows directory (or more specifically, the name of the folder in which the *\Windows\System32* folder can be found), usually *c:\windows*.

TEMP, TMP

The location where many programs will store temporary files. TEMP and TMP are two different variables, but they should both have the same value, usually set to *c:\Users\%USERNAME%\AppData\Local\Temp* (short name used to maintain compatibility with older DOS programs).

USERDOMAIN

The name of the domain to which the computer belongs (set by going to Control Panel → System → Computer Name → Change). If no domain is specified, USERDOMAIN is the same as COMPUTERNAME.

USERNAME

The name of the current user.

USERPROFILE

The location of the current user's home directory, which should be the same as HOMEDRIVE plus HOMEPATH, usually *c:\Users\%USERNAME%*.

WINDIR

The location of the Windows directory, usually *c:\windows*.

## sort

Sort text or the contents of text files in alphanumeric order.

### Usage

```
sort [/r] [/+n] [/m kilobytes] [/l locale]
  [/rec recordbytes] [/t [tempdir]]
  [/o outputfilename] [filename]
```

### Description

The sort command sorts text on a line-by-line basis. Each line of
the input is ordered alphanumerically and output to the screen (or
optionally, stored in a file). By default, sorting starts with the
character in the first column of each line, but you can change this
with the /+n option. sort is often used in conjunction with either
pipes or output redirection (both discussed earlier in this chapter).
That is, you might want to sort the output of another command,
and you will often want to redirect the output to a file so that it
can be saved. sort takes the following options:

/r

Reverses the sort order; that is, it sorts *Z* to *A* and then 9 to 0.

/+n

Sorts the file according to characters in column *n*.

/m kilobytes

Specifies the amount of main memory to allocate for the sort
operation, in kilobytes. The default is 90 percent of available
memory if both the input and output are files, and 45 percent of
memory otherwise. The minimum amount of memory sort will
use is 160 KB; if the available (or specified) memory is insuffi-
cient, sort will split up the operation using temporary files.

/l locale

Overrides the system default locale (see Control Panel →
Regional and Language Options). The "C" locale yields the
fastest collating sequence, and in Windows Vista, it is the
only choice.

/rec recordbytes

Specifies the maximum number of characters on a line (in a
record); the default is 4,096 and the maximum is 65,535.

/t *tempdir*
> Specifies the location of the directory used to store temporary files, in case the data does not fit in main memory (see the /m option). The default is to use the system temporary directory.

/o *outputfilename*
> Specifies a file where the output is to be stored. If not specified, the sorted data is displayed at the prompt. Using the /o option is faster than redirecting output (with the > symbol).

*filename*
> The name (and optionally, full path) of the file to sort.

## Examples

Display an alphabetically sorted directory (similar to dir /o):

```
C:\>dir | sort
```

Sort the contents of a file, *data.txt*, and store the sorted version in *results.txt* (the following four examples are equivalent, although the first is the most efficient):

```
C:\>sort /o results.txt data.txt
C:\>sort data.txt > results.txt
C:\>sort /o results.txt < data.txt
C:\>type data.txt | sort > results.txt
```

## time

Display or set the system time.

### Usage

```
time [/t | time]
```

### Description

Like date (discussed earlier in this chapter), time is essentially a holdover from the very early days of DOS when the user was required to enter the system date and time every time the computer was started. Now it's essentially included as a way to set the data from the command line; the preferred method is to use Control Panel → [Clock, Language, and Region] → Date and Time.

If you type **time** on the command line without an option, the current time setting is displayed, and you are prompted for a new one. Press Enter to keep the same date.

The time options are:

*time*

Sets the system time without a prompt. The format of *time* is *hh:mm:ss* [A|P], where:

*hh* Hours: valid values = 0–23.

*mm* Minutes: valid values = 0–59.

*ss* Seconds: valid values = 0–59.

A|P

A.M. or P.M. (for a 12-hour format). If a valid 12-hour format is entered without an A or P, A is the default.

/t Displays the current time without prompting for a new one.

## type

Display the contents of a text file.

### Usage

    type *filename*

### Description

The type command is useful if you need to quickly view the contents of any text file (especially short files). type is also useful for concatenating text files, using the >> operator.

## ver

Displays Windows version information.

### Usage

    ver

### Description

ver shows the version of Windows you're using. You can also find the Windows version at Control Panel → [System and Maintenance] → System tab, but it won't show you the revision number.

ver takes no options.

## where

Displays the location of files that match a filename.

### Usage

```
where /r /q [dir] /f /t [filename]
```

### Description

where will show you the location of files for which you're searching. It searches along your default path, although you can add directories to the default with the use of /r. It accepts wildcards such as * and ?. You can use the following commands with where:

/r  Searches for and displays the file, starting with the specified directory

/q  Quiet mode (no output, but it sets the exit code in %ERRORLEVEL%)

/f  Displays the matched filename in double quotes

/t  Displays the file size and last modified date and time for all matched files

### Examples

Display the location of all files named *eula.txt* along the default path:

```
where eula.txt
```

Display the location and file size, and last modified date and time, for all *.doc* files in the directory *\latest*:

```
where /r \latest /t *.doc
```

## whoami

Gets username and group information, security identifiers (SIDs), privileges, and logon identifier (logon ID) for the current user.

### Usage

```
whoami /upn /fqdn /user /groups /priv /logonid /all
/fo format /nh
```

### Description

You use whoami to get a variety of information about the currently logged-in user. You can use the following options with the whoami command:

/upn

Displays the username in User Principal Name (UPN) format. (Works only when the user is connected to a domain.)

/fqdn

Displays the username in Fully Qualified Distinguished Name (FQDN) format. (Works only when the user is connected to a domain.)

/user

Displays information about the current user along with the SID.

/groups

Displays group membership for the current user, the type of account, SIDs, and attributes.

/priv

Displays the security privileges of the current user.

/logonid

Displays the logon ID of the current user.

/all

Displays the current username and the groups the user belongs to, along with the SID and privileges for the current user.

/fo format
>   Specifies the output format to be displayed. Valid values are TABLE, LIST, and CSV. Column headings are not displayed with the CSV format. The default format is TABLE.

/nh
>   Specifies that the column header should not be displayed in the output. This is valid only for the TABLE and CSV formats.

## Examples

Display login ID and security privileges of the current user:

```
whoami /logonid
```

Display the current username, the groups the user belongs to, and the SID and privileges for the current user, in CSV output format, with no header displayed:

```
whoami /all /fo CSV /nh
```

## xcopy                                    \windows\system32\xcopy.exe

Copy files and directory trees (directories, subdirectories, and their contents).

## Usage

```
xcopy source [destination] [/a | /m] [/d[:date]] [/p]
    [/s [/e]] [/v] [/w] [/c] [/i] [/q] [/f] [/l] [/g]
    [/h] [/r] [/t] [/u] [/k] [/n] [/o] [/x] [/y] [/-y]
    [/z] [/b] [/exclude:filenames]
```

## Description

xcopy works like copy but provides more options and is often faster.

The xcopy options are:

source
>   Specifies the file(s) to copy; source must include the full path.

destination
>   Specifies the location and/or name of new files. If omitted, files are copied to the current directory.

/a   Copies files with the archive attribute set but doesn't change the attribute of the source file (similar to /m).

/c   Continues copying even if errors occur.

/d:*date*
    Copies only files changed on or after the specified date. If no date is given, copies only those source files that are newer than existing destination files.

/e   Copies all directories and subdirectories (everything), including empty ones (similar to /s). May be used to modify /t.

/exclude:*filenames*
    Specifies a file (or a list of files) containing strings of text (each on its own line). When any of the strings match any part of the absolute path of the file to be copied, that file will be excluded from being copied. Contrary to what you might expect, *filenames* does not actually list the filenames to exclude.

/f   Displays full source and destination filenames while copying (unless /q is specified); normally, only filenames are displayed.

/g   Allows the copying of encrypted files to a destination that does not support encryption; otherwise, such files are skipped.

/h   Copies hidden and system files also; normally files with the hidden or system attributes are skipped (see "Attrib," earlier in this chapter, for details).

/i   If a destination is not supplied and you are copying more than one file, assumes that the destination must be a directory. (By default, xcopy asks if the destination is a file or directory.)

/k   Duplicates the attributes of the source files; by default, xcopy turns off the read-only attributes.

/l   Displays files that would be copied given other options, but does not actually copy the files.

/m   Copies files with the archive attribute set, then turns off the archive attribute of the source file (similar to /a).

/n   Copies files using short (8.3) file- and directory names (for example, *PROGRA~1* instead of *Program Files*). Use this feature to convert an entire branch of files and folders to their short names.

/o   Copies file ownership and ACL information.

/p   Prompts you before creating each destination file.

/q   Quiet mode; does not display filenames while copying.

/r   Overwrites read-only files.

/s   Copies directories and subdirectories, except empty ones (similar to /e).

/t   Creates the directory structure but does not copy files; does not include empty directories unless /e is specified.

/u   Copies from the source-only files that already exist on destination; used to update files.

/v   Verifies copied files by comparing them to the originals.

/w   Prompts you to press a key before copying (useful in batch files).

/x   Copies file audit settings (implies /o).

/y, /-y
   Turns off or on (respectively) the prompt for overwriting existing files.

/z   Copies networked files in restartable mode.

/b   When copying a symbolic link (see "mklink," earlier in this chapter), copies the file as a link rather than making a couple of the source file (the default behavior).

The following are exit codes generated by xcopy. They can be tested in a batch file with ERRORLEVEL to determine whether the xcopy operation was successful.

0   All files were copied without errors.

1   No files were found to copy.

2   xcopy was terminated by Ctrl-C before copying was complete.

4    An initialization error occurred. Such an error would gener-
     ally be caused by insufficient memory or disk space, or an
     invalid drive name or syntax.

5    A disk-write error occurred.

## Examples

Copy all the files and subdirectories, including any empty subdirectories and hidden files, from *c:\foobar* to the root directory of *d:*

```
C:\>xcopy \foobar d: /s /e /h
```

# Index

## Symbols

* (asterisk), 131
\ (backslash), 131
\\ (backslashes, double), 131
. (dot), 131
.. (dots, double), 131
? (question mark), 131

## A

absolute paths, 24
accessibility options, 52
  Ease of Access Center, 52
  Microsoft Magnifier, 99
accounts, 97
  administrator accounts, 97
Add Hardware Wizard
  (hdwwiz.cpl), 87
Address Bar, 46
administrator accounts, 97
Aero, 1, 60
  Aero Glass, 1, 60
  hardware requirements, 12
  Live Taskbar Thumbnails, 54
  Vista versions including, 11
  Windows Flip 3D, 20, 60, 61
    activation, 36

All Programs menu, 56
  drag and drop moving of
    programs, 57
  Games, 58
  Startup, 57
ALLUSERSPROFILE
  environment
  variable, 158
Alt key
  keyboard shortcuts, 34
APPDATA environment
  variable, 158
applets, 48
  command-line, accessible
    from, 49
  (see also Control Panel)
applications
  Calculator, 98
  Character Map, 98
  Default Programs Control
    Panel, 99
  launching, 30, 31
  Microsoft Magnifier, 99
  Notepad, 100
  Program Compatibility
    Wizard, 100

We'd like to hear your suggestions for improving our indexes. Send email to
*index@oreilly.com*.